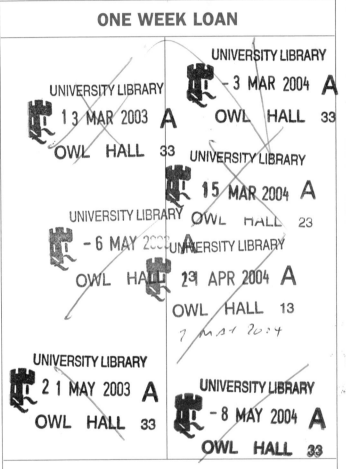

A NEW ERA IN US-EU RELATIONS?

To my mother and father

A New Era in US-EU Relations?

The Clinton Administration and the New Transatlantic Agenda

ANTHONY LAURENCE GARDNER

Ashgate
Aldershot • Brookfield USA • Singapore • Sydney

Published by
Ashgate Publishing Ltd
Gower House
Croft Road
Aldershot
Hants GU11 3HR
England

Ashgate Publishing Company
Old Post Road
Brookfield
Vermont 05036
USA

Reprinted 1999

British Library Cataloguing in Publication Data

Gardner, Anthony Laurence
    A new era in US-EU relations? : the Clinton administration
    and the new translantic agenda
    1. United States - Foreign relations - European Union
    countries - 1993 - 2. European Union countries - Foreign
    relations - United States
    I. Title
    327 . 7 ' 3 ' 04

    ISBN 1 85972 530 9

Library of Congress Catalog Card Number: 96-86726

Printed and bound by Athenaeum Press, Ltd.,
Gateshead, Tyne & Wear.

Contents

Acknowledgements

I am grateful to Professor Loukas Tsoukalis of the College of Europe and Professor George Bermann of Columbia Law School for having first sparked my interest in the European Union, and to the Council on Foreign Relations for having made my service at Director of European Affairs in the European Directorate of the National Security Council possible.

It was a pleasure to serve -- a second time -- under one of the most highly respected professionals in the US Foreign Service, Alexander Vershbow, Senior Director for European Affairs at the National Security Council. Despite the demands of his other responsibilities, particularly with regard to Bosnian peace and reconstruction, he took great interest in, and made a pivotal contribution to, the elaboration of the New Transatlantic Agenda. I was particularly fortunate, as well, to work with an extraordinarily able group of colleagues: one of them, Nelson Drew, tragically lost his life near Sarajevo while promoting the Bosnian peace to which he was so committed; many others, including Antony Blinken, Rosemarie Forsythe, Dan Fried, Mike Froman, Maryann Peters, Dan Poneman, Richard Schifter and Jonathan Spalter made my service at the NSC memorable. Frank Vargo, Deputy Assistant Secretary of Commerce for Europe, and Tim Richards, former Deputy Assistant US Trade Representative for Western Europe and the Mediterranean, played an important role in the elaboration of the New Transatlantic Agenda and enlightened me on several of the issues raised in this book. Finally, I wish to thank the excellent group of European Commission officials with whom I had the opportunity to collaborate: among them, Matthew Baldwin, Lodewyk Briet, Jim Currie, Jonathan Davidson, Jorge de Oliveira e Sousa,

Eckart Guth, Ove Juul Jorgensen, Astrid Schomaker, and Emanuela Silvestri.

A special word of thanks to Under-Secretary of Commerce Stuart Eizenstat, who is justifiably considered on both sides of the Atlantic as the most effective Ambassador to the European Union the United States has ever had: working with him and his able team at the US Mission in Brussels was a rare privilege. The fact that the Clinton Administration dedicated considerable diplomatic resources to the New Transatlantic Agenda was due, more than to any other single factor, to his energy, intellectual creativity and dedication to strengthening transatlantic relations.

Although I have sought in this book to describe the Clinton Administration's views and policies toward the European Union, the opinions expressed in this book are mine alone and should not be attributed to any member or part of the Administration. Moreover, it is self-evident that there is no single Administration view regarding the issues covered in this book: each Agency has its own views on specific matters, such as the Department of Defense on the Western European Union or the Department of the Treasury on Economic and Monetary Union There are, moreover, frequently many views within each Agency. Rather than attempt to examine each Agency's views scientifically, I have sought to describe in general terms how the Administration perceives the EU and its motivations for launching the New Transatlantic Agenda.

Finally, I wish to thank Michael Calingaert and Alejandra Mac-Crohon for having read an earlier version of this book and for having made many useful suggestions and corrections. The opinions expressed herein and the remaining errors are, of course, my own.

Foreword

I came to my post as US Ambassador in 1993 as an enthusiastic supporter of the European *Community* and left Brussels as an even more enthusiastic supporter of the European *Union* in 1996. The European Union (EU) serves the interests of the peoples of Europe, of the United States, and indeed of freedom loving people throughout the world. The EU serves as an important force for democracy, free markets and stability in western Europe among its 15 member states, and its positive impact on the newly emerging democracies of Central Europe and the Baltics is profound.

Additionally, the EU has an enormous effect on US trade and international commerce, and on the global economy as a whole. Together the 15 member states of the EU add up to the world's largest market, with 371 million people having a combined GDP of over $8.4 trillion -- slightly larger than the NAFTA market. Together the United States and the European Union account for nearly half of the entire world's output of goods and services and about half of total global trade. Considering both bilateral trade and the sales of production affiliates in each other's market, transatlantic commerce amounts to over $1.7 trillion annually! This is 50 per cent larger than transpacific commerce.

The United States has always supported, on a bipartisan basis, European integration, because of the belief that it fosters our national interest in seeing a stable, democratic and prosperous Europe. Tony Gardner's excellent book chronicles the development of this bipartisan effort, culminating in the Clinton Administration's negotiation with the EU of the New Transatlantic Agenda (NTA), which was signed at the US-EU summit in Madrid, Spain, in December 1995, and which has taken our bilateral relationship to an entirely new level.

There is no question in my mind that the NTA is the most significant step in US-EU relations since the beginning of the European integration movement in the 1950s. It recognizes the prime importance of the transatlantic relationship and moves it from a largely consultative and trade-oriented one to a more broadly-based action agenda intended to further our common political as well as economic goals around the globe. It demonstrates the continued commitment of the United States in the post-Cold War era to be a partner in the development of Europe's future. It belies any notion that the transatlantic relationship might atrophy in the absence of a common Communist foe. The NTA will enable the United States and the EU to harness our joint energies together across a wide range of political, economic, trade, diplomatic, science, health and private sector initiatives.

Tony Gardner's excellent book expertly describes the negotiation of the NTA and analyzes its early implementation. Some areas will show progress more quickly than others. Some are higher priority than others. Some are more susceptible to rapid completion than others. Not all can be worked on with equal vigor at all times. Disappointments and delays are bound to occur. But I am optimistic that the momentum will hold and that real progress is being made, and will continue to be made, in a number of very significant areas. I was privileged to play a major role in the development of the NTA, and I consider it the most important contribution I have been able to make while serving as US Ambassador to the EU and one of the most important in all my years of public service. One reason for my optimism is that we built an important "failsafe" feature into the NTA -- a follow-up mechanism to ensure that all these worthy goals and good intentions are not put on a shelf and forgotten. A US-EU "Senior Level Group" of sub-cabinet officials will prepare each US-EU summit to review progress on Agenda action items -- a semi-annual report card from the highest political level on how we are doing. This group and the working groups that support it constitute all-important "connective tissue" that will enable the NTA to have a real impact.

The other critical feature, which Tony describes in his book, is that the NTA set as a major goal "Building Bridges Across the Atlantic." This is the key to all the rest of the goals. Only if the private citizens of the United States and the EU understand, believe in, and participate in the transatlantic relationship will there be the public support necessary to make our other goals attainable.

The Transatlantic Business Dialogue is an excellent example of private sector engagement. The late great US Commerce Secretary Ron Brown first suggested this US-European business-government dialogue in December 1994 in Brussels and was soon joined by European Commission Vice President Brittan and Industry Commissioner Bangemann in his efforts to make the idea take shape. Late last year in Seville, Spain, the first Transatlantic Business Dialogue welcomed CEOs of more than 100 small, medium and large US and European companies. The business executives talked; the government officials listened; and we both learned a great deal about what we can most effectively do to further liberalize and facilitate our trade, by reducing regulatory barriers and duplicative product testing and certification; reducing and in some cases eliminating tariffs; requiring investment protection; and developing ideas on competing in third country markets. Since that time, the effort has involved an ever growing number of companies on both sides of the Atlantic, and 15 individual issue groups of US and European executives were formed. By the time of the June 1996 US-EU summit in Washington, the Transatlantic Business Dialogue had been accepted as the principal means of business input into governmental policy formulation to reduce commercial barriers. The summit leaders pledged to implement as many of their recommendations as possible. The Transatlantic Business Dialogue is not only a success story itself; it is also a working model of the kind of public-private interaction so necessary to a strong and vibrant transatlantic relationship.

With the NTA, the future of US-European relations, and indeed of the European Union, has never been brighter. One must not be misled by false litmus tests. On false standard is that the European Union is not becoming a "United States of Europe." Indeed it is not. Moreover, it is not likely to be so. Differences in national cultures, history and language are too great to permit this. I have been impressed at the strength and durability of the nation state and the degree of attachment to it. The people of Europe clearly still wish to make it their key point of identification, albeit within an integrated Europe. But it was not the purpose of the founders of the institution to have a federal nation state. Those who make this the test of success will always be disappointed. The European Union is and will be an entirely *sui generis* institution, and without precedent, neither a full-blown nation state nor simply another regional common market or customs union. It will be less than the former but much more the latter.

In truth, incredible progress has been made by the European nations in only four decades: a deep degree of economic integration with at least the commitment to increased political integration; functioning executive, legislative and judicial institutions; a common set of laws, the impressive *acquis communautaire*; a single market (although not yet fully complete); an increasingly open and deregulated market; and progress toward the creation of a European ethic. All of this has been accomplished with nation states, some of which have a history of almost a millennium, and historic antipathies to one another.

I have been an unabashed Euro-enthusiast because I believe that the European Union serves American as well as European interests. Problems arise from time to time with a stronger, more united independent voice on foreign policy issues, as we see with our differences over the EU's "critical dialogue" with Iran, which we believe has utterly failed to produce any positive changes in Iranian behavior, or the EU's Cuba policy, which we are concerned might reward the Castro regime without sufficient signs of genuine political and economic changes. These problems, though, are more than offset by the fact that on the big issues we are always likely to have more convergence than divergence because we share the same values, outlook, history, culture, and commitment to expand democracy and free markets around the world.

The stronger voice the EU has already assumed as a trade negotiator is more than balanced by having a clear focal point for negotiations which bind all member states, and by the fact that the EU shares the US commitment to a strong multilateral trading system and to the World Trade Organization (WTO), open markets, free trade, and deregulation, all of which enhance our common interests. The competition a stronger European economy provides to US business in third-country markets is more than counter-balanced by the additional US exports, the added profits to US-owned companies in Europe, and the stability and absence of social tension in Europe that results from a healthier European economy.

The New Transatlantic Agenda is not an end point, but the beginning of a deeper relationship. In my personal opinion, this will not be complete until we seal our futures even more tightly together over the years as the EU more fully develops its mechanisms in the foreign policy area and as we move inexorably toward a genuine, transatlantic economic framework of fully free, unimpeded trade and commerce. The NTA provides a means to develop a stronger, global US-EU partnership, but it does not guarantee the EU that role. The EU will earn its role by being able to act effectively and quickly as our partner in the rest of Europe and in the world.

No one is better able to describe and analyze the US-EU relationship than Tony Gardner. For it was Tony who served as the key EU expert on President Clinton's National Security Council staff from 1994 to 1995 and who was a seminal figure in the development of the NTA. Without Tony's support, suggestions, advice, and counsel, and finally, his determination to press forward with the NTA with members of the White House staff, the NTA would have been still-born, depite all of our efforts in Brussels. In this important and well-written book, Tony combines a scholar's analytic eye with a practitioner's views and experience.

I want to conclude this foreward with one cautious note: the people of the United States must be more educated about the European Union. Few, even well educated private citizens and senior policy makers, know much about it. This is a danger in terms of building support for a closer US-EU relationship. One of the basic problems is that very little about the EU is written in almost any daily newspaper or magazine published in the United States or is seen on American television. Even though the future of Europe, in my opinion, can best be observed from Brussels, where the interplay of member states occurs, US publications try to cover Europe from London, Paris or Frankfurt. Major US news publications have no news bureaus or even full-time correspondents based in the "capital of Europe."

Tony Gardner's book will help fill this void, not just for the student of modern European history or of world trade, but for influential citizens throughout the United States. Perhaps it will even convince some of the US press to open bureaus in Brussels!

Ambassador Stuart E. Eizenstat
Under Secretary of Commerce for International Trade

Washington D.C.
July 1996

List of acronyms
used in the text

AAMA	Association of American Motor Vehicle Manufacturers
ACEA	Association de Constructeurs Européens d'Automobiles
AID	Agency for International Development
APEC	Asia Pacific Economic Cooperation
CAP	Common Agricultural Policy
CEE	Central and Eastern Europe
CFSP	Common Foreign and Security Policy
COCOM	Coordinating Committee for Multilateral Export Controls
EC	European Community
ECHO	European Community Humanitarian Aid Office
ECSC	European Coal and Steel Community
EDU	European Drugs Unit
EEC	European Economic Community
EPC	European Political Cooperation
EU	European Union
EURATOM	European Atomic Energy Community
EUROPOL	European Police
FBI	Federal Bureau of Investigation
FDA	Food and Drug Administration
FDI	Foreign Direct Investment
GATT	General Agreement on Tariffs and Trade
GATS	General Agreement on Trade in Services
IGC	Inter-Governmental Conference
ITA	Information Technology Agreement
KEDO	Korean Energy Development Organization
MAI	Multilateral Agreement on Investment
MFN	Most Favored Nation
MRA	Mutual Recognition Agreement
NAFTA	North American Free Trade Agreement
NHTSA	National Highway Transportation Safety Administration
NIS	New Independent States

NTA	New Transatlantic Agenda
OECD	Organization for Economic Cooperation and Development
OEEC	Organization of European Economic Cooperation
OSCE	Organization for Security and Cooperation in Europe
PFP	Partnership for Peace
SME	Small and Medium Sized Enterprises
TABD	Transatlantic Business Dialogue
TAFTA	Transatlantic Free Trade Area
TRIPS	Trade Related aspects of Intellectual Property Rights
UN-ECE	United Nations Economic Commission for Europe
UNSCOM	United Nations Security Council Observer Mission
USTR	US Trade Representative
WEU	Western European Union
WTO	World Trade Organization

Part One

The background to the New Transatlantic Agenda

1 Introduction

> We do not regard a strong and united Europe as a rival but as a partner...capable of playing a greater role in the common defense, of responding more generously to the needs of poorer nations, of joining with the United States and others in lowering trade barriers, resolving problems of commerce and commodities and currency, and developing coordinated polices on all economic and diplomatic areas.

President John F. Kennedy, Speech in Philadelphia, 4 July 1962.

> I believe our best partner as we look toward the 21st century for prosperity and peace is a Europe united in democracy, in free markets, in common security.

President William J. Clinton, Speech in Berlin, 13 July 1994.

The United States and the European Union (EU) are seeking to open a new era in the history of their relationship by committing themselves to a transatlantic partnership based on common objectives and joint actions. Until the Transatlantic Declaration of 1990, US-EU relations were largely characterized by *ad hoc* consultations focussed on a variety of trade issues. These consultations were supplemented during the subsequent five years with a formal mechanism for dialogue on a broad range of economic and political issues. At the US-EU Summit in Madrid on 3 December 1995, President Bill Clinton, Spanish Prime Minister and President of the EU Council Felipe Gonzalez, and European Commission President Jacques Santer announced a New Transatlantic Agenda (NTA) to forge even closer ties between the United States and the European Union by implementing *coordinated policies* on a broad range of economic, political, security, humanitarian, environmental, scientific and educational issues.

The initiative differs from previous incantations about common transatlantic values and traditions: rather than being inspired by nostalgia, it is a concrete blueprint for action in response to the fundamental truth of today's interdependent world that many of the most important challenges facing the United States and the European Union cannot be addressed satisfactorily by either acting alone. These challenges -- such as international crime, terrorism, environmental destruction, poverty and disease -- are transnational in scope and require human and financial resources which exceed those at the disposal of the US, the EU or national capitals at a time of increasing budgetary austerity.

In order to understand how this initiative came about, and in particular why Washington was prepared to commit considerable diplomatic resources to it at the highest levels despite increasing commitments to resolving conflicts in Bosnia, the Middle East and Northern Ireland, it is necessary to review the reasons why the Clinton Administration formed a positive overall assessment of the European Union and the potential for a strengthened US-EU partnership. Many of these reasons are similar to those which led the United States to provide crucial support for the early stages of European integration.

2 The origins of US support for European integration

During the presidencies of Truman, Eisenhower and Kennedy, the US provided economic inducements to, and occasionally applied political pressure on, Europe to create the institutions of regional collaboration -- such as the Organization of European Economic Cooperation (OEEC), the European Coal and Steel Community (ECSC), the European Atomic Energy Community (EURATOM) and the European Economic Community (EEC) -- which have profoundly shaped Europe's present identity. Indeed, of all the factors which have contributed to this identity, none has had a more profound effect than the Marshall Plan which explicitly tied reconstruction aid to European integration.[1]

The crucial support of the United States during the early years of European integration prompted Walter Hallstein, first President of the European Commission, to declare upon taking office in January 1958 that "There is a saying that the Americans are the best Europeans, and there is much truth to that."[2] In that same year the United States became the first nation to establish formal diplomatic relations with the European Communities.

The United States fathered European integration primarily to achieve political, rather than economic, objectives; it calculated that the numerous political advantages of European integration would outweigh any injury which its exporters might suffer due to the trade diverting effects of a customs union and the EEC's conclusion of preferential and discriminatory trade agreements.[3] It sought to promote Franco-German reconciliation in order to address the root causes of European instability which had prompted two American military interventions this century. The pooling of sovereignty in Europe in critical sectors such as coal and steel -- the backbone of military power -- would mark the end of the great balance of power game which had characterized European history for centuries. The unification of Western Europe was seen as a first step to the unification of the European continent west of the Soviet Union on the foundations of democracy and the free market and, subsequently, to the elimination of Europe's division into two ideologically incompatible blocs. American postwar leaders were concerned that the survival of these values at home ultimately depended on their survival in Europe. Just as the European Community (EC) helped underpin democracy in Germany and Italy, so did it later play the same role in Greece, Spain and Portugal.

The United States also considered that rapid integration was essential to generate the economic revival necessary to raise living standards and strengthen democratic institutions of government, relieve part of Washington's burden of increased spending on defense against the Soviet military threat and greater aid to the Third World to combat Communist influence, and benefit the US balance of trade by generating increased demand for American exports. These objectives were supplemented by the "inner faith" of Americans in their own history of union, federalism, and the mingling of peoples from different cultures and traditions.

Criticism in Europe of American leadership, particularly with regard to the Vietnam War, the increasingly independent foreign policies pursued by European states toward Russia and the Arab world[4] following the thaw in East-West relations at the end of the 1960s, growing transatlantic economic competition and fears that the creation of the EEC was erecting barriers to American businesses in Europe and discriminating against them in third country markets led to a reevaluation of this benign view of European integration during the Johnson and Nixon Administrations. The enormous enthusiasm which had existed in the 1950s and early 1960s for the prospect of a United States of Europe gave way to disappointment that the Community was in reality operating as a mere customs union, apparently devoid of idealistic political aspirations.[5] Growing domestic economic difficulties and rapid growth rates in Europe lowered the tolerance of US administrations to pay an economic price, particularly in the form of EU discrimination against US farm exports, for supporting European integration.

Henry Kissinger's support for European integration belied his abiding faith in the nation-state as the key player in international politics and his paternalistic view of Europe's importance in global affairs. His "Atlantic Charter" proposing a new relationship between the United States and Europe within the Atlantic Alliance stated this in undiplomatic language:

4

Diplomacy...is essentially conducted by traditional nation-states. The United States has global interests and responsibilities. Our European allies have *regional interests.*[6]

Influenced by his study of the Congress of Vienna and Count von Metternich's mastery of the balance of power game, Kissinger believed that the fragmentation of Europe was desirable because it afforded the United States opportunities to exert greater leverage with its allies and thereby maintain unquestioned leadership of the Alliance.

Relations between the United States and the European Union became closer during the Ford and, in particular, the Carter Administrations. President Carter became the first US president to officially visit the headquarters of the Commission in Brussels in January, 1978. Later that year, European Commission President Roy Jenkins conducted a well-publicized trip to Washington during which he was given a warm reception at the White House.[7] Declaring unqualified support of the United States for European integration, Carter later illustrated his administration's serious regard for the Community by welcoming the participation of the President of the European Commission at annual summits of the G-7 and by expressing understanding for European Political Cooperation (EPC), despite the fact that it might result in positions contrary to US policy.

By the end of the Carter Administration and into the beginning of the Reagan Administration, US-EU relations took a turn for the worse. The Community's June 1980 Venice Declaration on the Middle East calling for a Palestinian homeland and Palestinian participation in Arab-Israeli peace talks diverged sharply with US policy. Moreover, Washington condemned the Community for its timid reaction to the Iranian hostage crisis and its refusal to collaborate in US retaliation against Moscow -- particularly the ban on European subsidiaries of US firms to supply equipment for the construction of the Siberian pipeline -- following the suppression of Solidarity in Poland and the Soviet invasion of Afghanistan.[8] Festering economic disputes regarding the Common Agricultural Policy (CAP), the Community's subsidies for Airbus and oilseed production, its ban on hormones in beef, and its level of compensation for the US expected trade loss from Spanish and Portuguese accession to the Community, as well as growing concern in Washington about the potential for anti-US discrimination in the 1992 program, exacerbated transatlantic tensions.

The pendulum swung back again toward a more positive assessment of European unity (and the expressions of its independent identity) during the Bush Administration. The tumultuous events in Central and Eastern Europe

(CEE) in 1989 demonstrated to the administration the important role that an integrated Western Europe could play in terminating the division of the continent and stabilizing its eastern half. The President declared:

> we believe a strong, united Europe means a strong America...a resurgent Western Europe is an economic magnet, drawing Eastern Europe closer, toward the commonwealth of free nations.[9]

At the world economic summit of G-7 heads of state and government in Paris in July, 1989, Bush called upon the industrialized countries to recognize the European Commission's leadership role in organizing financial and technical assistance to Central and Eastern Europe. Partly in recognition of the Commission's enhanced role and prestige, the administration upgraded the diplomatic status of its delegation in Washington by accrediting its permanent representatives to the White House, rather than to the State Department like other heads of international organizations.[10]

Moreover, unlike his predecessor, Bush granted European Commission President Jacques Delors head of state treatment on his visits to Washington. Notoriously conscious about protocol, Delors had been insulted by the low-level reception he had received in Washington during the Reagan Administration. Although his demand for all the trappings of an "official" visit -- including a twenty-one gun salute and military review on the South Lawn of the White House, an overnight stay at Blair House, and a press conference with the President -- were not satisfied during his trip to Washington in mid-June 1989, he was hosted at a White House lunch with President Bush and leading members of his administration.[11]

Nevertheless, US policy toward the European Community continued to be troubled by trade disputes related to the negotiations within the General Agreement on Tariffs and Trade (GATT) and by anxieties that Europe's efforts to define a common security and defense identity would ultimately endanger the central role of the North Atlantic Treaty Organization (NATO) within the Alliance. Several leading members of the Bush Administration mistrusted Delors and relations between him and President Bush were never warm.[12]

When considered against this background, the Clinton Administration deserves to be judged as the most enthusiastic supporter of European integration since the Kennedy Administration.

This enthusiasm has stemmed in part from the personal rapport which Clinton and Delors quickly established, particularly during the former's trip to Brussels in January 1994. More significantly, however, the Clinton Administration has taken the view that European integration is, on balance, very positive for Europe and the United States in economic *and* political terms. Although it has been as <u>vigilant</u> as its predecessors in defending American interests against protectionist or discriminatory trade policies of the European Union, the Administration has rejected earlier fears that the 1992 Single Market Program would create a Fortress Europe. The Administration has sought to build on the consultations between the European Union and the United States since the signing of the 1990 Transatlantic Declaration by promoting a true collaborative partnership.

Notes

1   The early years of US support for European integration are well described in Pascaline Winand, *Eisenhower, Kennedy, and the United States of Europe*, St. Martin's Press 1993.

2   As quoted in Reginald Dale, "Marshall to Maastricht: US-European Relations Since World War II," *Europe* June 1995, p. 12.

3   Roy Ginsberg, "US-EC Relations" in *The European Community and the Challenge of the Future*, ed. Juliet Lodge, St. Martin's Press 1989, pp. 265-266.

4   In a communiqué of 15 December 1973, the EC called on all sides to take into account the legitimate rights of the Palestinians. The Euro-Arab dialogue between members of the Arab League and the EC dates from 1974.

5   See René Schwok, *US-EC Relations in the Post-Cold War Era: Conflict or Partnership?*, Westview Press 1991, pp. 28-29.

6   Henry Kissinger, *Years of Upheaval*, p. 153 citing "Fourth Annual Report to the Congress on United States Foreign Policy, 3 May 1973," *Public Papers of the Presidents, Richard Nixon*, US Government Printing Office 1973 [141], pp. 402-405.

7   René Schwok, *US-EU Relations in the Post-Cold War Era: Conflict or Partnership?*, Westview Press 1991, p. 33.

8   At the 1982 Versailles summit meeting of the G-7, Treasury Secretary Donald Regan had clashed with President Delors over European participation in the construction of the Siberian gas

pipeline, East-West trade and a European proposal for concerted central bank intervention in world currency markets. Axel Krause, *Inside the New Europe*, Harper Collins 1991, pp. 291-3.

9   Speech at Boston University on 21 May 1989, as quoted in *Ibid*, p. 294.

10   Ibid, p. 295. The Community's office in Washington was elevated to the diplomatic level of a "delegation" in 1971. René Schwok, *US-EU Relations in the Post-Cold War Era: Conflict or Partnership*, Westview Press 1991, p. 29.

11   Axel Krause, *Inside the New Europe*, Harper Collins 1991, p. 295.

12   According to one of the closest observers of Delors, "The pragmatic Baker understood the importance of getting on with Delors. But Bush never felt comfortable with Delors and sometimes saw the EC as a mere trade club. Some of those who had Bush's ear liked neither Delors nor his organisation. Brent Scowcroft, the national security adviser, thought Delors anti-NATO; Carla Hills, the trade representative, saw him as a French agent; and Nicholas Brady, the treasury secretary, viewed EMU as a threat to the dollar." Charles Grant, *Delors: Inside the House That Jacques Built*, Nicholas Brealey 1994, p. 166.

3   The Transatlantic Declaration

Informal US-EU consultations date back to 1974. In 1976 it was agreed that the head of state or government of the country holding the Community's presidency would meet once during his six month term with the US president and that the Foreign Ministry of that country would keep Washington informed both before and after meetings of political directors on European Political Cooperation. Following serious transatlantic disputes regarding East-West relations in the early 1980s, annual meetings were initiated between Troika[1] political directors and the Assistant Secretary of State for European Affairs on the margins of the UN General Assembly. In September 1986 further structure was added to transatlantic consultations: the US and the EU agreed that the foreign minister of the country holding the Community's presidency would visit Washington at the beginning of each year and that the Troika political directors should meet during each presidency with their US counterparts at the Under-Secretary level.[2]

In addition to these growing levels of transatlantic consultation, *ad hoc* consultations between members of the US cabinet and their EU counterparts took place between 1982 and 1990. These meetings were usually held following the annual December NATO summit in Brussels and involved the Secretaries of State, Commerce, Agriculture and Treasury, together with the Trade Representative, on the US side, and the President of the European Commission, together with the respective Commissioners, on the European side.

The transformation of Europe in the second half of the 1980s made clear that these mechanisms for US-EU consultation needed to be considerably strengthened. The 1986 Single European Act facilitated EU decision-making by introducing majority voting, in place of a unanimity requirement, in some areas. Even more important, the disintegration of the Soviet bloc dramatically increased the likelihood that Europe might become unified and harness its increased political and economic power to play a global role.

One month after the fall of the Berlin Wall in November 1989, Secretary of State James Baker visited Berlin and called for closer transatlantic cooperation to keep pace with European integration and institutional reform:

> [w]e propose that the United States and the European Community work together to achieve, whether it is in treaty or some other form, a significantly strengthened set of institutional and consultative links.[3]

This echoed President Bush's earlier declaration, in response to a proposal by President Delors, that the US was prepared to develop with the Community "new mechanisms of consultation and cooperation on political and global issues."[4] Implicit in Baker's initiative was the concern that the Community might develop policies and institutions incompatible with American interests if the process of European integration were not accompanied by improved transatlantic dialogue.

The initiative resulted nearly one year later in the Transatlantic Declaration. The document repeats a great deal of familiar poetry about the transatlantic attachment to common values, principles and traditions, especially democratic government, human rights and market economics. More significantly, however, it established a mechanism for regular transatlantic consultations between heads of state, foreign ministers, other cabinet members, political directors and experts, either in a trilateral format (representatives from the US Government, the European Commission and the country holding the presidency of the EU Council) or in a troika format (representatives from the US Government, the European Commission and preceding, current and subsequent EU presidency countries). In addition, the Declaration also formalized exchanges between the European Parliament and the US Congress.

Held between the presidents of the United States, Commission and Council, once per six-month EU presidency and alternating between Washington and Europe (normally in the capital of the current presidency country), the US-EU summits were to provide the central direction to the entire process of consultation. The summits have varied in usefulness according to the personal chemistry between the leaders. Although relations between Presidents Bush and Delors were always correct, the two leaders did not develop the same intellectual rapport as that which existed between

Presidents Clinton and Delors, who enjoy immersing themselves in the details of public policy.

The summits held in accordance with the 1990 Transatlantic Declaration have usually been isolated events which do not build on one another. As such, the summits have been criticized as show pieces primarily intended for consumption by the media. Nevertheless, they have served an important function by reinforcing the Commission's credentials to represent Europe when speaking with the United States. Moreover, they have regularly forced the bureaucracies on both sides of the Atlantic to define positions for their political masters on key transatlantic issues. Although US-EU relations are rarely characterized by crisis, regular summits are necessary to ensure that they receive adequate attention and that occasional disputes, typically over trade and US efforts to impose its laws extraterritorially, are managed before causing serious transatlantic frictions. It may be hoped that the New Transatlantic Agenda will breathe new purpose into the summits and that ongoing consultations through the Senior Level Group of high-ranking US and EU officials, described in Chapter 6, will help provide direction and ensure more substantive agendas.

In accordance with the Transatlantic Declaration, the US Secretary of State meets with all of the foreign ministers of the EU on the margins of the UN General Assembly meeting in the fall of each year; as they are normally accompanied by several advisers each, these meetings tend to be a choreographed exchange of prepared remarks, rather than an informal dialogue. In the spring of each year and on an *ad hoc* basis, however, the Secretary also meets in a less formal setting with the foreign minister of the EU presidency country and the EU commissioner in charge of relations with the United States. From Washington's perspective, this trilateral format has been preferable to the troika format because it maintains a role for the Commission and thereby guarantees continuity in US-EU consultations.

Although the Transatlantic Declaration called for semi-annual meetings at cabinet level, the practice fell into disuse since December 1991, partly because their agendas focussed on topics related to the Uruguay Round (and agriculture in particular) which were being discussed intensively elsewhere. Under the Clinton Administration, cabinet-level consultations have been substituted by semi-annual sub-cabinet meetings alternating between Brussels and Washington at which Joan Spero, US Under-Secretary of State for Economic and Business Affairs, and Peter Tarnoff, Under-Secretary of State for Political Affairs, have met with their counterparts in Directorate-General I (external relations) of the European Commission. The meetings held between Joan Spero and Horst Krenzler,

Director-General for relations with the US and other advanced industrial countries, have proven particularly useful because they provide advance warning of trade disputes.

The format of these meetings permits substantive discussion and identification of issues requiring resolution at a higher level. The recent practice of holding meetings between political directors / assistant or deputy assistant secretaries of state before the sub-cabinet meetings, has further improved the latter's focus and effectiveness. Within the US Government, these meetings facilitate inter-agency coordination between the Department of State, the Office of the United States Trade Representative (USTR), the National Economic Council, National Security Council, Department of Commerce, and the Department of the Treasury.

The purpose of semi-annual consultations held in accordance with the Transatlantic Declaration at the level of political directors/assistant or deputy assistant secretaries of state have been to identify areas of shared interest and recommend specific actions at the experts level, such as the formulation of joint policies and the implementation of parallel démarches. The consultations at experts level (deputy assistant secretaries or heads of bureau) have covered a vast array of topics, including UN affairs, nuclear non-proliferation, human rights, terrorism, consular affairs, and the Organization for Security and Cooperation in Europe (OSCE), as well as numerous geographical areas, including Latin America, Russia and the New Independent States (NIS), the former Yugoslavia, Central and Eastern Europe, the Middle East, Africa and Asia.

Several lessons may be drawn from the consultations conducted under the framework of the Transatlantic Declaration. The clearest lesson is that the quality of the consultations varies according to the EU presidency country's management abilities and commitment to strengthening US-EU relations. During the Presidency of The Netherlands in the second half of 1991, the Hague often provided Washington with advance copies of the agendas of EPC meetings, transmitted Washington's input (without identifying it as such) to the Member States and briefed Washington on the results of these meetings.[5] Similarly, the Luxembourg Presidency in the first half of 1991 played an important role in keeping US and European policy toward Iraq in step. The degree of cooperation between Washington and the French EU presidency in the first half of 1995 was rather less satisfactory. The presidential elections in March and the entry into power of a new leadership team distracted the bureaucracy of the Quai d'Orsay from its EU obligations; although France had pledged at the beginning of its presidency to build on the preceding German presidency's work to improve

US-EU consultations, it delayed or blocked every concrete initiative to achieve this objective because of a Gaullist hyper-sensitivity about Washington's *droit de regard* over European affairs. By contrast, the enthusiasm of the Spanish Presidency in the second half of 1995 for reinvigorating transatlantic relations and its energetic efforts, along with the Commission, to forge intra-European consensus on the New Transatlantic Agenda (occasionally achieved by presenting the Council with *faits accomplis*) enabled US and EU negotiators to elaborate a major initiative within only five months after the end of the French Presidency.

The consultations held under the Transatlantic Declaration also show that consultations held in the trilateral format are more effective at promoting dialogue because they maintain continuity in the identity of the participants. In order to strengthen its power within the EU bureaucracy, and increase its international profile in particular, the Commission has sought to hold as many meetings as possible with the United States in this format. Washington has been a willing partner in this objective because of the conviction that, compared to the Council, the Commission has broader perspectives on international affairs which are more likely to be compatible with US interests and has greater ability to strike compromises between the Member States and the EU institutions.

In order to be effective, US-EU consultations must feature a two-way exchange of information in order to produce results. Consultations under the Transatlantic Declaration achieved only modest results because they were, until the launch of the New Transatlantic Agenda, merely briefings given by US participants for their European counterparts for which the former obtained little in return. Effective consultations also require that the different levels of interaction are coordinated so that the actors at each level are aware of the others' activities; meetings at each level must also be better linked over time so that they build on one another and have a clear, ultimate objective. All of this can only occur in the context of a structured dialogue whose momentum is ensured by commitment at the highest levels.

Even a few years after the launch of the Transatlantic Declaration it was evident that new and improved mechanisms for consultation were needed. Chancellor Helmut Kohl, the primary proponent of such mechanisms, believed that only a transatlantic of greater structure and intensity could prevent a gradual shift in Washington's attention toward Asia and domestic economic problems. In November 1992 he proposed that relations between Europe and the United States be embodied in a comprehensive treaty. Although Washington was not prepared to engage in so ambitious an exercise, it acknowledged the need for greater structure, more continuity between US-EU summits and greater emphasis on pragmatic collaboration. Eager to avoid the uncomfortable position of having to choose between Washington, its premier international ally, and Paris, its essential partner in the promotion of European integration, Bonn wished to find a flexible mechanism for US-EU policy coordination between summits as a way of defusing transatlantic policy differences before they were aired publicly. The transatlantic search to "deepen" the Transatlantic Declaration resulted in the launch of the three "working groups" by Clinton, Delors and Kohl at the US-EU Summit in July 1994 in Berlin. Before turning to these groups in Chapter 5, it is necessary to describe the Clinton Administration's policy toward the EU and to explain why it sought to strengthen US-EU relations.

Notes

1   The Troika consists of representatives from the preceding, current and subsequent EU presidency countries.

2   René Schwok, *US-EU Relations in the Post-Cold War Era: Conflict or Partnership?*, pp. 32-35.

3   James Baker, "A New Europe, A New Atlanticism: Architecture for a New Era," Press Office of the Department of State, Berlin, 12 December 1989, p. 6, as quoted in René Schwok, *US-EC Relations in the Post-Cold War Era: Conflict or Partnership*, Westview Press 1991, p. 170.

4   In an interview granted to *The Wall Street Journal* in February, Delors had floated the idea of new US-EU "partnership" which would consist of dialogue on political and security issues, in addition to trade. Axel Krause, *Inside the New Europe*, Harper Collins 1991, p. 294.

5   In practice, Washington rarely provided The Hague with any input. But the American Embassy in The Hague was regularly briefed on Presidency and Troika trips and on meetings concerning the former Yugoslavia.

4 The Clinton Administration and the European Union

A few months after President Clinton assumed office, *The Economist* wrote that his foreign policy advisors "look less sympathetic to the EC than their predecessors" and that Clinton "treats Western Europe as less urgent than Russia, Bosnia or the Middle East." Anthony Lake, the President's National Security Advisor, it alleged, had never heard of the Transatlantic Declaration.[1] Other commentators claimed that neither Secretary of State Warren Christopher nor Stephen Oxman, the Assistant Secretary of State for European Affairs, was an expert in European affairs.[2]

Such observations were, perhaps, triggered by the fact that Clinton had won the presidential election largely on his pledge to focus on domestic, rather than foreign, policy and that the Administration had taken pains during its first year in office to stress its interests in *both* Asia and Europe, rather than pre-eminently in the latter, as some European may have liked. In fact, fears about an American "drift" from Europe have been a familiar European refrain following almost every change of administration; such fears eventually dissipate after a ritual invocation by the new administration of America's "marriage vows" with its European "bride." The number of experts on the EU within any US administration has always been rather limited, perhaps no more than several dozen spread between the State Department, the Commerce Department, the Office of the Trade Representative, National Security Council and the Central Intelligence Agency. What has varied considerably, however, has been the effectiveness of the US Mission to the EU and the political clout in Washington of its ambassador.

The Clinton Administration has formed a strongly positive assessment of the EU despite two factors which might have produced a different result. First, several leading political appointees might well have brought with them an outdated perception of the EU dating from their last service in government during the Carter Administration, well before the EU had expanded its competencies and improved its cohesiveness under the 1986 Single European Act and the 1991 Treaty on European Union ("The Maastricht Treaty"). Second, due to a one-quarter cut in the budget and staff of the White House, including the National Security Council, to satisfy a pledge that the President had made during the campaign, the White House has increasingly come to rely on the short-term detachments of Foreign Service Officers and military and civilian personnel from the Pentagon. The arrangement has enabled the White House to cope with serious under-staffing while keeping those on detachment off the White House staff list and budget because they are paid and employed by their sponsoring agencies. The professional experiences of these individuals are far more likely to have been in the arena of politics and security than in the arena of economics and trade and their perceptions of Europe are far more likely to be NATO-centric than EU-centric.

Nevertheless, several key members of the Administration have been convinced that continued European integration is good for Europe and the United States and that closer US-EU cooperation is essential to address satisfactorily many of the most pressing challenges of the post-Cold War world. Stuart Eizenstat, formerly US Ambassador to the EU and subsequently Under-Secretary of Commerce for International Trade, was able to draw upon his close friendships at the highest levels of the Administration to ensure that the European Union receive high priority attention in US foreign policy. Working primarily with Secretary of Commerce Ron Brown, Deputy National Security Advisor Samuel Berger, Assistant Secretary of State Richard Holbrooke, the Bureau of Regional Affairs in the State Department and the Senior Directors for European Affairs in the National Security Council, Eizenstat succeeded in crafting a strong EU element to the President's first trip to Europe in January 1994.

The President's speech in Brussels was intended, and succeeded, to dispel fears in Europe about the Administration's commitment to transatlantic relations following the collapse of the Soviet empire. "The new security must be found in Europe's integration," Clinton said, "an integration of security forces, of market economies, of national democracies." During the Berlin US-EU Summit later that year, he declared that the EU is an "indispensable ally" of the United States in addressing virtually every significant foreign policy challenge. These statements reflected the conclusion of the Administration, in stark contrast to the philosophy underlying Kissinger's approach to Europe, that further European integration is compatible with, and even supportive of, transatlantic links.

Some of the reasons for this conclusion are identical to those which inspired US post-war leaders. Integration is still seen as a means of creating a European identity, and thereby combating Europe's tendency toward

16

introspection) it is also seen as a guarantor against the emergence of a fragmented Europe prone to internal conflict. This process of integration has been promoted by a growing body of European law, supreme over conflicting national law and enforceable in national courts, which has served as the foundation of a single market in which goods, services, people and capital circulate freely. Moreover, the Community's Structural and Cohesion Funds, which finance infrastructure projects in economically disadvantaged areas, have helped overcome the disparities in development and wealth which continue to divide Europe.[3]

Echoing similar preoccupations of America's post-war leaders, some EU watchers in the Administration concluded that Germany (particularly after reunification) would inexorably dominate an intergovernmental Europe, regardless of the benign nature of its policies, because of its size, population, geographic position and economic and political weight. With the collapse of the Iron Curtain and the reestablishment of Germany's traditional trading and cultural links, it was foreseeable that Central Europe would reenter Germany's economic sphere of influence. It was important that the reemergence of German power occur within a European context to promote pan-European, rather than purely, German objectives. Chancellor Kohl had himself diplomatically called for a "European roof" over a "German House" and, similarly, for a "European Germany" rather than a "German Europe." Expressing the same thought rather less delicately, French Prime Minister Edouard Balladur observed that unless Germany were constrained by the provisions governing political and economic union in the Maastricht Treaty it would:

> act as it desires, without taking heed of its neighbours or its partners, without being constrained by any set of common European rules in its role as a military, economic, financial and monetary power in the centre of the continent.[4]

From Washington's perspective, the pooling of sovereignty at Community level facilitates the integration of a reunified Germany within Europe and magnifies the weight of the small Member States, such as the Benelux, which have traditionally been internationally-minded and supportive of strong transatlantic links.

The importance which the United States attaches to its relations with the Community reflects the limits on the utility of bilateral relations with EU Member States when seeking to achieve transatlantic foreign policy objectives. France's traditional reluctance to support foreign policy initiatives of American origin, regardless of their merits, places obvious constraints on Washington's dialogue with Paris. The self-imposed isolation of the United Kingdom from Europe also diminishes the value of London as a key interlocutor on Europe. Only in Bonn does Washington find the combination of economic power, strategic vision and common interests. Yet Germany's history and desire to avoid a backlash of resentment from its European partners prevent Bonn from using fully the political powers at its disposal.

The growing importance after the end of the Cold War of global issues not strictly related to traditional security concerns -- such as environmental degradation and transnational organized crime -- has increased the attractiveness of the EU and, in particular, the European Commission as an interlocutor of the United States. As Professor Alberta Sbragia has trenchantly observed, the rise of a "global agenda" has led Washington to seek partners with a "global mentality":

> As a global power, the United States seeks to transact business with other like-minded protagonists. London, Paris and Bonn are all trapped in some ways by their histories. The Commission, on the other hand, is a more compatible partner. It has many of the psychological and intellectual characteristics expected in the executive branch of an entity with jurisdiction over a huge market, relations with much of the developing world, and the ability to circumvent to at least some extent Europe's embeddedness in the past.[5]

Although the importance of bilateral cooperation is declining in some areas, this certainly does not mean that Washington is likely to ignore the utility of concentrating its diplomatic strategy on EU Member States when it is useful to do so. This is particularly true in trade where divergent interests among Member States and between several Member States and the Commission offer fertile ground for the United States to promote its interests. Among the numerous recent examples, three figure prominently:

- The Administration has moved swiftly to sign bilateral 'open skies' agreements with Austria, Belgium, Denmark, Finland, Germany, Luxembourg and Sweden, rather than negotiating a US-EU accord as urged by EU Commissioner for Transport Neil Kinnock.[6] These agreements, allowing airlines in one country to fly to any airport in the other and to pick up passengers there to fly to any other point in the world, have placed pressure to follow suit on France, Greece, Italy, Spain, Portugal and, most importantly because of its 40 per cent share of the transatlantic air market, the United Kingdom (which already signed a 'mini-deal' with the United States in July 1995).

- The Administration signed a bilateral agreement with Germany in June, 1993, whereby Germany agreed not to apply the terms of the EU's Utilities Directive which discriminate against non-EU suppliers of telecommunications equipment; in turn, it excluded Germany from Title VII trade sanctions keeping the EU out of certain US public procurement opportunities.

- Despite support for the EU's Common Foreign and Security Policy (which in turn implies rationalization of the European arms industry, interoperability of national armed forces and the promotion of common European armaments production programs), the Administration has conducted vigorous export promotion campaigns urging (successfully) the United Kingdom and Netherlands to purchase US Apache helicopters and urging (unsuccessfully) Spain to purchase US Blackhawk helicopters over European competition (Westland and Eurocopter).

All three examples, of course, involve efforts by the United States to obtain commercial advantages. But the first two form part of an overall effort to liberalize transatlantic trade and to eliminate commercial restrictions in Europe; as such, they may be expected to yield considerable benefits for European companies and consumers as well. The third example is rather different because it involves an effort to win a zero-sum game even at the cost of further distorting the playing field of international commercial competition. However regrettably, high-pressure government-sponsored export promotion has been widely practiced by many countries, and it is unlikely that this will change as long as there are strong domestic pressures on governments to protect employment in specific sectors and as long as these governments are not willing to curb such practices through international agreements.

Notwithstanding a natural tendency to deal with Member States rather than with the Union when it is advantageous to do so, the Clinton Administration has been been an enthusiastic supporter of European integration. During his trip to Brussels in January 1994, the President sought to put to rest persistent European doubts about his commitment to Europe. The trip achieved its mission. *The Economist*, which had been so skeptical about the President's commitment to Europe only several months previously, changed its tune:

America's rationale for favouring European togetherness is simple: convenience and burden-sharing...A strong, confident Europe should also make a better partner than a weak, divided one -- better able to *spread stability eastwards* or to *promote free trade*.[7]

This analysis was correct.

Set forth below are some of the principal reasons why the Clinton Administration considers the EU as an ally in the objective of liberalizing markets and trade in Europe and worldwide; why it on balance supports Economic and Monetary Union (EMU); and why it considers the EU as an ally on a wide variety of foreign policy issues despite the obvious weaknesses of the EU's Common Foreign and Security Policy (CFSP).

The EU as ally in liberalizing markets and trade

In economic terms, it has been clear to the Clinton Administration that European integration is a positive development for Europe and the United States: the European Community, and the European Commission in particular, have been among Washington's most important allies in promoting liberalized trade in Europe and worldwide.

The Commission has played a central role in creating a single market that is a level playing field for all participants. The European subsidiaries of American companies have been faster to realize and exploit the potential of this market than their native competitors. In forging a single market, the Commission has used EC antitrust laws to combat restrictive or abusive trade practices by private firms, expose public monopolies in protected sectors to competition, and limit (although with uneven success) competition-distorting forms of public financial aid to troubled firms.

One of the reasons that the Commission has been able to pursue a free market agenda so effectively within Europe is that it has, until recently, conducted its work as an elite body insulated from the pressures of protectionist public opinion. Greater transparency, particularly in the formulation of administrative rule-making procedures, and accountability in the Union's decision-making would go a long way toward addressing the Community's "democratic deficit," but may impinge on the Commission's free market vocation by giving greater weight to such opinion.[8]

The Commission's liberalizing policies have achieved particularly notable results in the field of telecommunications, the world's fastest growing industry. Entrenched monopolies in the Member States unsuccessfully sought to prevent the Commission from opening telecommunications services and terminal equipment to free competition. More recently, the ineluctable force of technological progress and the evolution of world markets persuaded them to support the Commission's long campaign to liberalize voice telephony, the most profitable sector of telecommunications, by 1998. Other protected sectors, such as energy and postal services, have not evolved as quickly, but the Commission continues to press for their progressive liberalization.

Although the Community occasionally reflects the protectionist sentiments prevailing in several Member States, most notably in France, it has made significant progress toward eradicating Europe's cartel culture and guiding Europe toward free trade in the non-agricultural goods and services sectors. Every round of EU enlargement has limited France's ability to use Community institutions as megaphones for its own economic and political interests. One of the critical reasons for Washington's enthusiasm for the accession of Austria, Finland and Sweden was that they would reinforce the Anglo-Saxon free trade camp, with the notable exception of their highly protected agricultural markets, as well as the Atlanticist orientation of the Community.[9] This was of particular concern in light of France's increasingly aggressive campaign in favor of stronger EU commercial defense instruments, such as anti-dumping and safeguards, and of EU challenges to US trade policy instruments before the World Trade Organization (WTO).

The Commission has also played an important role in liberalizing trade worldwide. US-EU trade negotiations would have taken even longer, and more of them would have failed, had it not been for the Commission's role as the Community's exclusive trade negotiator. Some US officials who have been through these marathon negotiations complain about the Commission's inflexibility as a negotiating partner: the Commission must have a mandate in order to negotiate, but once it has a mandate its ability to exercise discretion is limited. It is true that the Commission strongly resists modifying a position once it has been hammered out as a compromise between the divergent views of the EU's Member States. Before this compromise has been reached, however, the Commission is instrumental in limiting the influence of protectionist sentiment within the Member States and in crafting a distribution of gains and losses among them which makes them prepared to accept EU concessions.

Moreover, the Commission's exclusive competence as trade negotiator has responded to Henry Kissinger's famous complaint that the United States does not have a single telephone number to call when it wants to talk to "Europe". This convenience played a key role in enabling the United States and Europe to hammer out the compromises on agriculture, aerospace and public procurement which unblocked the stalemated Uruguay Round negotiations. Although the Commission may prove to be a weaker trade negotiating partner of the United States as a result of an advisory opinion in

1994 of the European Court of Justice[10] that the Commission must share competence with EU Member States in negotiations concerning the "non-traditional" areas of services and intellectual property rights, the Commission's residual trade negotiating powers remain considerable.

Economic and Monetary Union

The Commission has championed plans for Economic and Monetary Union (EMU) in order to perfect the single market by reducing transaction costs, eliminating exchange rate risks and securing the benefits of low inflation. These plans will have consequences for the US-EU bilateral relationship, as well as for international monetary policy.

With regard to the bilateral relationship, the austerity measures which are being implemented to meet the "convergence criteria"[11] of EMU may, over the short term, have a deflationary impact by dampening European economic growth and, in turn, demand for American imports. A single European currency, moreover, may develop over the longer term into a viable reserve asset drawing international capital away from dollar-denominated investments, thereby placing upward pressure on interest rates and complicating efforts at deficit reduction and the management of monetary policy.[12] By eliminating the need for foreign exchange transactions internally, moreover, a monetary union may create a "dollar overhang" by rendering much of the dollar reserves of Member State central banks superfluous. The liquidation of these dollar reserves without close US-EU coordination would clearly lead to currency volatilty and the dollar's depreciation. Finally, if the dollar lost its leading role as a reserve currency, New York City might be unable to retain its role as the world's financial capital over the longer term.

With regard to international monetary policy, it is also possible, though unlikely, that a single European currency may diminish European interest in multilateral consultations on monetary policy (e.g. through the G-7) by lowering European vulnerability to international exchange rate volatility. It is more likely, however, that EMU will complicate, rather than simplify, the process of coordinating monetary and foreign exchange intervention among the United States, Europe and Japan. In the past, exchange rate accords could be negotiated discreetly between a small number of government officials in order to avoid currency speculation and volatility. EMU will result in the proliferation of actors on the European side who would be involved in the negotiation of exchange rate accords -- Member State governments' representatives in the Council, the Commission, the European Central Bank and, in certain circumstances, even the European Parliament -- and may therefore make such accords more difficult to achieve.[13] What is

22

certain is that European monetary union and the creation of a European Central Bank will affect representation within the G-7 and will marginalize the role of Canada and non-EMU EU countries, such as Italy and possibly the United Kingdom.

As under previous administrations,[14] the US Treasury of the Clinton Administration has been virtually silent with regard to EMU. This silence may be partly ascribed to the skepticism of certain officials that a single currency will ever come about and to the view that US stakes in, and ability to influence the outcome of the debate regarding, EMU are marginal. Following the EU's clear reaffirmation in early 1996 of its intention to proceed with Economic and Monetary Union in 1999 among "hard-core" countries satisfying the Maastricht "convergence criteria", and in light of severe austerity programs implemented by those countries to achieve that objective, the US Treasury has gradually become convinced that EMU will indeed occur. Of the risks for the United States outlined above, the most significant, in the eyes of leading Clinton Administration officials, has been that high European interest rates and austerity programs may further exacerbate unemployment and depress economic growth and consumer demand in Europe, thereby dampening global trade and reducing American exports.[15] Despite such concerns, the Clinton Administration has formed a marginally positive view of EMU on the ground that, despite possible deflationary effects over the short term, EMU is likely to unleash the single market's maximum wealth-creating potential and to create significant opportunities for American business over the longer term.

The EU's Common Foreign and Security Policy

Unlike his predecessor, President Clinton has repeatedly stressed that the United States favors a Europe which is not only economically integrated, but which has a security and defense identity as well. Only then will Europe be able to fulfil President Kennedy's vision of a second pillar in the transatlantic alliance and to take on its full share of the burden of protecting and expanding democracy, stability and prosperity throughout the world. As Secretary of State Warren Christopher has declared:

> the United States looks to Europe to be a strong partner for the United States and a capable actor on the world stage. Of course, the choice of mechanisms is for EU members themselves to decide. But the United States has a clear interest in Europe's continued integration and its enhanced ability in foreign and security policy.[16]

The EU's nascent Common Foreign and Security Policy (CFSP) is therefore greeted positively in Washington, despite two dangers which lie at opposite extremes. On the one hand, the common policy could be *too effective*: it could have a high 'common denominator' and might diverge from US objectives, thereby making them harder to achieve. On the other hand, the policy might be *not effective enough*: it could further diminish the coherence and speed of Europe's actions on the world stage.

Like the looser system of European Political Cooperation which it replaced, CFSP has succeeded in reducing the potential for friction between Member States; the habit of collaboration encouraged by CFSP has largely resulted in modest, albeit useful, initiatives, such as election monitoring (in South Africa, Russia and the Middle East), a 'stability pact' for Central and Eastern Europe (establishing a framework for the resolution of disputes concerning borders and minorities), coordinated voting of Member States in the United Nations and other international organizations, and responses to humanitarian disasters in the Third World.

The risk that CFSP may pose problems for the United States by becoming too effective is largely theoretical at present and is likely to remain so for a long time to come. Europe's inability to respond effectively to the Bosnian conflict, contrary to the claim of Luxembourg Foreign Minister Jacques Poos in 1991 that the "hour of Europe" had arrived, has made particularly evident that CFSP is still taking its first tentative steps.

The EU administration of Mostar is frequently invoked in Brussels as a CFSP success story. But its record there has been rather uninspiring: despite spending over ECU 100 million and stationing several hundred monitors, known as the "ice-cream men" because of their white uniforms and their inability to enforce order,[17] the EU was unable to convince the Bosnian Croat authorities in the western half of the divided city to let people pass freely from the Bosnian eastern half (despite the existence of a "Bosnian-Croat Federation"). The EU scored an important victory in August 1996 when it brokered a deal between Mostar's Croats and Muslims whereby the former would accept the results of the June 1996 municipal elections won by a Muslim-Serb coalition. Although the deal temporarily salvaged the EU mission to reconstruct and reunify Mostar, it remains to be seen whether it will be respected and whether the EU will remain in Mostar well beyond the September 1996 elections scheduled in Bosnia.

Moreover, there is little indication that the EU is developing a capability to deal with problems in its own back-yard. The fact that it was the United States, rather than the EU, which calmed Greek-Turkish tension over the islets of Imia in the eastern Aegean in February 1996 demonstrated again the weakness of CFSP.[18] For the time being, there is little question that Washington considers it more efficient to work through bilateral channels,

24

particularly with Bonn, Paris and London, to achieve its foreign and security policy objectives.

To many observers in the United States, the Common Foreign and Security Policy simply lacks credibility. This is not only because CFSP has failed to generate any high-profile policies in the security field. It is also due to CFSP's modest resources, its lack of an organizational identity and its inability to present a common face to Washington. Fraser Cameron, Counsellor for CFSP in Directorate-General IA of the European Commission, has summed up well the poor impression which the European Union makes when it sends large delegations to Washington to meet with US officials:

> Sometimes we have a table like this and we have 15, 16 or 17 people on the European side and Warren Christopher rather isolated on the other side. It does not make us look actually very credible to the US and other interlocutors.[19]

The Commission spends a great deal of energy gaining the right to represent and speak for the EU at as many international organizations as possible, regardless of whether its real influence justifies a seat at the table.[20] This policy has been the source of considerable irritation in Washington because it increases the number of participants without improving the substance of meetings and because the Commission usually (but not always) echoes the voices of its Member States. Some Member States of the EU are frequently uncomfortable with being represented in foreign policy assemblies *exclusively* through the Commission: with their continued aspirations to be regional, if not global, powers, France and the United Kingdom, jealously guard their sovereign right to be represented in their national capacities.[21]

When Washington seeks to engage the EU on foreign policy, it also tends to be bewildered by the confusing array of actors with overlapping fields of competence: the staff of Directorate-General IA in the European Commission under Commissioner Hans Van den Broek; the foreign policy staff in the Secretariat of the Council of Ministers; the Political Directors of the 15 Member States who meet regularly to coordinate policy; the Troika; and the Foreign Ministry of the Member State holding the EU Presidency in six-month rotation. To some officials in Washington, negotiating with the EU must indeed seem like 'shaking hands with a multiheaded octupus...'[22]

Even in Washington the 15 EU Member States rarely present a common face. Reflecting the European Commission's external trade negotiating competence, the Commission's Delegation in Washington has become a credible interlocutor of the Office of the Trade Representative, the Department of Commerce and the State Department on transatlantic trade

25

issues; due to the reflexes of several Member States (particularly the United Kingdom and France) to pursue independent foreign policies and to maintain large embassies in Washington in order to seek privileged connections to the US bureaucracy, however, the Delegation is rarely able to speak on behalf of the EU on issues other than trade.[23] The Delegation has occasionally found the US Government to be a useful ally in cajoling the 15 Member States to present their *démarches* together through the EU. In January 1995, for example, the White House agreed -- over French reluctance -- to the Delegation's proposal that EU Commissioner Sir Leon Brittan and Foreign Minister Juppé should together meet with National Security Advisor Anthony Lake to discuss a range of transatlantic trade and political issues. Although France held the presidency of the EU Council at the time, the first reflex of the Quai d'Orsay was to use Juppé's visit to Washington exclusively as an occasion for addressing Franco-American relations.

From Washington's perspective, the greatest danger posed by CFSP is that it will be sufficiently binding on the Member States to prevent them from engaging in certain bilateral initiatives with the United States without being effective enough for the EU to act as a true partner of the United States on the world stage. According to Stuart Eizenstat, former US Ambassador to the European Union:

> When we go to individual Member States to try to have bilateral initiatives, we are going to be increasingly told 'no, we have a Common Foreign and Security Policy, we would like to cooperate, but only within the overall competence of the Union.' And then when we go to the Union, we find that the Union does not have the institutional framework to make that policy a reality.[24]

That institutional framework consists of a "three pillar" structure granting different institutions overlapping competencies over foreign policy and providing for complex and time-consuming decision-making mechanisms. The division of competencies between the Community's institutions over foreign and security policy is not always clear, particularly since many economic and social issues have a direct impact on this policy: while trade issues (including economic sanctions) lie in the hands of the Commission and are subject to one set of decision-making mechanisms enshrined in the Treaty of Rome, issues of crime and drugs lie -- like CFSP -- primarily in the hands of the Council of Ministers (e.g. the Member States) and are subject to a different set of decision-making mechanisms.

The "pillar" dealing with CFSP provides for an intricate procedure, prone to result in agreements at the level of the "lowest common denominator," by which EU foreign ministers may decide that certain areas of foreign and security policy merit joint action which is binding on the Member States; on the basis of instructions set by their heads of government in the European Council, EU foreign ministers may decide by unanimity that a certain matter should be the subject of joint action and may again decide by unanimity that certain decisions regarding implementation should be taken by qualified majority vote. In light of this complexity and difficulty of achieving unanimity, one might well conclude that "The Maastricht structure might almost have been designed to make a common foreign policy impossible."[25]

The weaknesses of CFSP may be partly cured as a result of the 1996 Inter-Governmental Conference (IGC) aimed at improving EU decision-making procedures and reforming EU institutions before the next round of enlargement. The Progress Report of Carlos Westendorp, chairman of the Reflection Group on the IGC, presents a menu of options for improving the effectiveness of CFSP by centralizing foreign and security policy functions: these options include the creation of an analysis, forecasting and planning unit within the Council Secretariat; departure from the unanimity principle on limited matters; and the creation of the position of spokesperson or Coordinator for Common Foreign and Security Policy.

But it is open to question whether even such measures would address the fundamental problem for CFSP's failure, as identified by European Commission President Jacques Santer at the World Economic Forum in Davos: "a lack of political will to work together as a Union, to share responsibility and the costs of joint action."[26] From Washington's perspective, CFSP is likely to remain weak because the interests of EU Member States in foreign and security policy remain profoundly divergent and because many Member States are unwilling to cede control over it.

Further enlargement will, of course, compound the problem; but it is not the source of this failure of political will. Although Austria, Finland and Sweden have long traditions of neutrality and will likely resist participating for the foreseeable future in a common EU defense policy or military venture, they appear committed to taking full part in the Union's foreign policy. They have become observers of the Western European Union (WEU) and members of the Partnership for Peace (PFP), the program which has given 27 countries a kind of associate membership in NATO. Moreover, it is unlikely that the next wave of members -- including Poland, the Czech Republic, and Hungary -- will be less than fully committed to CFSP.

The inherent weakness of CFSP reflects the different geographies, histories and cultures of EU Member States, including the Six which signed the Treaty of Rome. These divergences will only fade with the passage of time and the growing together of Europe's peoples through the habit of cooperation. As long as these peoples continue to consider themselves

French or German or British, rather than Europeans, CFSP will remain principally a formalism.[27]

Upon his election as president of France in May 1995, Jacques Chirac urged that the EU should, as a priority objective, work toward strengthening CFSP. But his intention to do so appeared to have been premised on the condition that the common policy had to be articulated by France and followed by all other EU Member States. Chirac's record during his first months in office suggested that he favors European solidarity principally when it serves France's interests and that, while France is free to criticize its partners, it should not be criticized in turn. With the exception of the United Kingdom, with which France is increasingly cooperating on foreign policy and security, Chirac does not appear to take seriously the aspirations of France's partners to pursue independent foreign and security policies. His pursuit of perceived French national interests regardless of the positions of fellow EU Member States may weaken the prospects of CFSP even further.

Recent events demonstrate this risk. When Italy voted (along with nine other EU Member States) in mid-1995 for a United Nations resolution deploring the continuation of nuclear testing in the Pacific, Chirac cancelled a meeting with Prime Minister Dini to protest that a fellow member of NATO and the WEU failed to show solidarity with France. Yet France had earlier shown little European solidarity by announcing the resumption of nuclear tests without warning, let alone consultation. Nor had it shown solidarity when it successfully excluded Italy from participation in an "enlarged" Contact Group on Bosnia despite the latter's significant contributions to the peacekeeping effort which Rome felt, with sympathy from many leading officials in the Clinton Administration, justified a seat at the table. Laboring under the illusion that the United States had the power to command members of the Alliance what to do, Rome sought to enlist Washington's aid to reverse French opposition to Italian participation.

France has also failed to show solidarity with its other European partners. President Chirac did not consult with Chancellor Kohl before scrapping France's compulsory military service and making deep cuts in its armament programs, despite the traditionally strong links between Paris and Bonn and the obvious repercussions of such decisions on the German internal political debate on national defense issues. In April 1996, President Chirac dispatched his Foreign Minister to the Middle East to negotiate a cease-fire rather than work through the EU's Troika system to help resolve the conflict between Israel and Lebanon. Such intra-European squabbles highlight the inability of Europe to speak with one voice.

As the Maastricht Treaty itself recognizes, an effective EU foreign policy ultimately depends on an effective *security and defense policy*. It is

28

in this area that the gap between the EU's aspirations and rhetoric, on the one hand, and capabilities and political will, on the other hand, is particularly striking. Most European countries are reducing their military budgets, shortening or eliminating periods of compulsory military service and the size of their armed forces because of the greater cost of increasingly sophisticated moderrn weaponry and budgetary austerity programs imposed by the run-up to EMU. None of the EU Member States has sufficient long-range airlift capabilities or intelligence assets, especially satellite imagery, to project and sustain power for extended periods beyond the European theater.

While remaining separate from the EU, the WEU is intended to be the EU's military arm: the Maastricht Treaty designated it "an integral part of the development of the Union, to elaborate and implement decisions and actions of the Union which have defence implications."[28] The Clinton Administration has been supportive of the WEU, on the condition that it complement the central role of NATO in transatlantic defense cooperation. This support reflects the expectation that, by contributing to a European defense identity, the WEU will contribute to a greater willingness in Europe to assume greater responsibility for its own defense. According to US Ambassador to NATO Robert Hunter:

> The cold-war argument that the alliance needed centralized military direction, and that a robust WEU could interfere, no longer applies. We support the WEU as a means of preventing the renationalization of defense. The WEU will help to focus minds on security, and thus aid the EU's attempts at common foreign and security policies...the more the European allies help themselves, the more Congress is likely to pay for transatlantic defense.[29]

But the WEU's modest means have prevented it from playing more than a modest role. With a staff of 80 and a planning cell of 40 in Brussels, a security studies institute in Paris and an operation at the Torrejon Air Force Base in Spain to gather satellite intelligence, the WEU has some autonomous ability to gather information and propose action. But as it has no forces of its own, it depends on troop contributions from Member States to conduct military operations.[30] Furthermore, even the WEU's participation in naval operations enforcing sanctions against Serbia along the Adriatic ('Operation Sharpguard') and the Danube have relied on NATO infrastructure and command and control. In light of NATO's primacy in European defense, the WEU has decided to limit its role to what are known as the 'Petersberg Tasks' after a declaration of the same name: peacekeeping, facilitating humanitarian aid and rescues, and using combat forces for crisis management.

29

The backbone of a true European defense capability will be an independent European defense industry. This does not yet exist: many Member States, particularly in France, Germany and Italy, continue to support their national champions by protecting them from foreign ownership or influence and awarding them major defense contracts without following procedures for open and transparent public procurement; moreover, the free trade and competition rules in the Treaty of Rome do not apply to the defense sector. As a result, the European defense industry is segmented on national lines, with poor economies of scale and is, therefore, uncompetitive. In addition to wasting roughly ECU 11 billion a year in European taxpayer's money, according to one European Commission report,[31] this situation has contributed to European purchases of conventional arms from the United States which far outstrip purchases by the United States from European Member States from one another.[32]

Although steps have been taken to encourage intra-European defense cooperation through joint ventures and cooperative research and development programs, the revitalization of Europe's defense industry will depend in large part on its future restructuring and rationalization (through mergers and acquisitions) and exposure to free competition (open public purchasing procedures, stricter application of state aids rules and the removal of barriers to the free movement of goods). The European Commission has urged rapid progress to achieve these objectives.

The recent decision by President Chirac to privatize the Thomson defense and electronics group and to encourage the merger of Aerospatiale, France's largest state-owned aerospace company, with Dassault Aviation are certainly important steps in the direction away from the protection of national champions and toward the creation of a European armaments industry. At the time this book was being written, Alcatel was considering a bid for Thomson, a step which would later enable the former to merge the defense businesses of the latter and the UK's General Electric Company (GEC) to create a European defense electronics giant. There are also other cross-frontier mergers and cooperative ventures under way which will promote restructuring and rationalization in Europe's defense sector. The merger of the missile businesses of British Aerospace and Matra may help to form the nucleus around which Europe's future missile industry will coalesce. Despite its lengthy delays and cost overruns, Britain, Germany, Italy and Spain appear committed to proceeding with the Eurofighter aircraft. Several countries, including France, are also involved in a cooperative venture to build a large turbo-prop military transport plane to replace Europe's US-built Lockheed Hercules aircraft.

In light of the serious social costs of restructuring and "down-sizing", particularly at a time of sluggish economic growth, however, there is little likelihood that Europe will develop a radically more efficient defense industry in the near future. It is also unlikely that Europe will be prepared to make significant expenditures to duplicate existing NATO assets at a time of budgetary austerity. Indeed, European defense budgets, periods of military service and capabilities have been dramatically cut back over the last six years. The conclusions to be drawn from this are as clear to policy makers in Washington as they are to those in Europe: the material requirements for a meaningful European security and defense policy will be lacking for a long time to come.

The easiest way of building a European security and defense identity "on the cheap" is to permit the WEU to use NATO assets. Seeking to encourage a true European pillar in the Atlantic Alliance, the Clinton Administration has effected a major foreign policy shift by agreeing to permit the WEU to borrow *collective* NATO assets for "out of area" missions in which the United States chooses not to participate. According to this Combined Joint Task Force concept, these collective assets would be separable but not separate from NATO. But, as France frequently points out, the practical consequences of this policy are limited as long as the definition of what constitutes "collective assets" is defined restrictively. Indeed, France's recent rapprochement with NATO, short of joining its integrated military command, may indicate that the Elysée recognizes that NATO will remain for the foreseeable future the only way of guaranteeing American engagement in Europe and that it is not economically feasible to duplicate NATO assets.[33]

Although it is possible to consider President Chirac's recent offer to Germany to share nuclear strategy (without nuclear weapons) as a first step toward a true common European defense policy, that day is likely to be a long way off. The clear motivation behind the offer -- to cloak renewed French nuclear testing in a European mantle to defuse vocal European opposition -- and the inherent difficulty of "sharing" decision-making on matters regarding national survival indicate that the *force de frappe* is unlikely to provide the catalyst for a common defense policy.

The evident weaknesses of CFSP do not mean that Washington considers Brussels to be irrelevant on matters of foreign and security policy, however. To the contrary, it is evident that many EU Member States are gradually becoming less unilateralist and more Europeanist. Naturally, the European reflex is slower in countries -- such as the United Kingdom and France -- which have histories and continuing aspirations of being global powers. But actions taken by individual countries contrary to a European consensus or policy are no longer taken for granted; they must be justified.

Despite the inability of CFSP to respond to "hard" security threats, moreover, the EU has already proven that it can make a valuable contribution toward addressing "soft" foreign policy issues. The clearest example of this has been the Commission's use of its exclusive trade competence to conduct policies which help strengthen the multilateral trading system and stabilize the former Soviet Bloc and the Third World. Another example is the Commission's growing role in humanitarian relief efforts to respond to famine, disease and environmental degradation. In the post-Cold War period, poverty and humanitarian crises will generate the main threats to the First World: authoritarianism and religious fundamentalism, civil wars, regional conflicts, terrorism and mass migration. From Washington's perspective, the European Union is an essential partner in dealing successfully with these challenges to world stability.

Common foreign policy interests

The EU as ally in stabilizing the former Soviet Bloc

The Economist was correct to emphasize that Washington considers a united Europe to be better able than a weak and fragmented Europe to "spread stability eastwards." One of the central themes of the Clinton Administration's foreign policy has been the concept that free trade promotes open economies and democracy and that, in turn, democracy promotes stability. In his 1994 State of the Union Address, the President declared:

> Ultimately, the best strategy to ensure our security and to build a durable peace is to support the advance of democracy everywhere. Democracies don't attack each other.[34]

By enhancing its trading relations with CEE and the NIS, and by providing considerable financial assistance, technical aid, and support for democratic political structures in the region, the EU contributes to the stabilization of the European continent. In a speech in Madrid on 2 June 1995, Secretary of State Warren Christopher paid tribute to the EU's role:

> The EU does more than open its markets to the new economies of the region.... It provides incentive and shelter for the development of civil societies that are the surest guarantee for stability and security. And it encourages the resolution of ancient enmities today in Central Europe as after World War II between France and Germany.[35]

Enlargement is one of the key ways in which the EU promotes free trade, democracy and stability in Europe. Bulgaria, the Czech Republic,

Estonia, Hungary, Latvia, Lithuania, Poland, Romania, Slovakia and Slovenia have already applied for membership in the EU. Although enlargement negotiations will not even begin until after the conclusion of the Inter-Governmental Conference and accession of some or all of these applicants is unlikely until after the year 2000, the European Union has already been contributing to the political and economic stabilization of Central and Eastern Europe. In anticipation of their eventual accession to the EU, the Visegrad countries have been carrying out a major effort of market reform. Much of the existing commercial legislation in the Czech Republic, Hungary and Poland has been brought into conformity with EU standards.

Following on the commitment of EU heads of state and government at the Essen Summit in December 1994, the European Commission presented a comprehensive "white paper" in May 1995 on the steps which the potential applicants for EU membership from Central and Eastern Europe must take to conform to the Single Market, particularly with regard to state subsidies and competition rules. While the adoption in the east of the EU's laws and regulatory models primarily benefits European companies, it also benefits the European affiliates of US firms, improves the climate for American investment and may stimulate demand for US exports by promoting economic growth.

The EU has projected stability eastward in several other ways. It has provided the bulk of the world's financial aid and technical assistance for legal and market reforms in CEE and integrated the region into trans-European transport and communication networks. Moreover, the EU has contributed to the CEE's sense of inclusion in Western institutions: the participation of CEE heads of state at the EU Summits in Essen in December 1994 and Madrid in December 1995, as well as the subsequent participation of CEE foreign ministers once every six months in the General Affairs Councils of EU foreign ministers, have given CEE leaders a voice in the construction of the EU and a sense that they are making progress toward their ultimate goal of accession.[36]

Even more important, the EU has contributed to the region's economic renewal by opening its markets to CEE exports. Whereas total US imports of CEE goods has declined since 1989, EU imports have increased dramatically over the same period. Nearly 80 per cent of CEE exports go to the EU, but only 5 per cent to the United States.[37] Critics of the EU's policy toward Central and Eastern Europe have pointed out, with justification, that instead of actively supporting the region's newly acquired independence through free access to the EU market, Brussels has too frequently caved in to Member State pressures to impose anti-dumping duties and other trade restraints against the CEE's most competitive exports, particularly steel, textiles and agricultural products.[38] Nonetheless, the Association ("Europe") Agreements which the EU has signed with Bulgaria, the Czech Republic, Hungary, Poland, Romania, the Slovak Republic and the three Baltic states, provide for free trade in industrial goods, including in the "sensitive" sectors of steel and textiles as of 1 January 1997 and 1998, respectively. These agreements are also significant because they provide for CEE adoption of a considerable part of the *acquis communautaire* (accumulated body of EU law), closer political contacts with the EU, and a clear track toward accession.

Critics within the Administration, particularly in the Office of the US Trade Representative, point out that these agreements give European companies an export advantage vis-à-vis their American competitors; as tariff barriers to trade between the US and CEE persist, the United States is indirectly encouraging US firms to invest in European affiliates rather than at home. These critics also point out that the EU's partial preferential trade areas (excluding sensitive products such as agriculture) with CEE and the NIS -- as with several countries bordering on the Mediterranean, and possibly with Mercosur (a customs union between Argentina, Brazil, Paraguay and Uruguay), Mexico and South Africa -- risk undermining the multilateral trading system. When compared to the political benefits which have flowed from the EU's leadership in the economic and political stabilization of CEE, however, the costs to US exporters to CEE and to the multilateral trading system appear relatively modest. In any event, US exporters to CEE will cease to suffer discrimination when the region eventually accedes to the EU and adopts the latter's low tariff wall.

Perhaps the EU has made its greatest contribution to the stabilization of CEE by simply acting as a model of peace and prosperity which the countries of the region wish to imitate. It has also made a significant contribution by diminishing residual Central and Eastern European concerns about German domination: convinced that an increasingly integrated Europe has anchored Germany in a peaceful democracy and has subsumed German aspirations within pan-European objectives, the region is prepared to accept the reemergence of German monetary, commercial and cultural influence.

The Clinton Administration has enthusiastically supported the early accession of Central and Eastern Europe into the EU. Its policy toward the region springs from the same sentiment expressed by Lionel Barber of the *The Financial Times*:

> If the European Union has a mission for the millenium, it is enlargement to the east. Integrating the former communist countries of central and eastern Europe with the capitalist west is the stuff of which history and heroes are made.[39]

Eastward enlargement would help ensure that the region develops a democratic, free market orientation and, just as significantly for the United States at a time of severe budgetary austerity, that the EU bears most of the financial burden associated with this development. The EU has already carried out similar tasks in Greece, Spain and Portugal, all of which have evolved from political instability and military rule before their accession into stable democracies today. The discipline of EU membership would help contain the reemergence of ancient disputes regarding frontiers and ethnic minorities in Central and Eastern Europe, as well as the danger that these might in turn destabilize Western Europe by spreading conflict or triggering migration.

Eastward enlargement is also desirable from Washington's perspective because it is likely to contribute to the pressures already placed by the Uruguay Round Agreement on the EU further to reform the CAP which has poisoned transatlantic trade relations for decades. Poland is destined by its political and strategic importance and strong ties to Germany to be among the first of the Central and Eastern European countries to enter the EU. But its entry would pose an acute problem: with the agricultural sector accounting for 6% of total GDP and 25% of total employment, Poland would strain the EU budget if it qualified for CAP benefits.

The Clinton Administration has not expressed an opinion as to *when* the EU's eastward enlargement should occur, nor as to the modalities of accession, as these are technical internal EU issues over which the United States has little influence. From Washington's perspective, however, clear progress in negotiations toward enlargement before the end of the century would relieve some of the pressure from Central and Eastern Europe for an early eastward enlargement of NATO and would therefore preserve Washington's latitude in managing NATO expansion to minimize frictions with Moscow and avoid undermining Russia's democratic development. This is particularly true with regard to the Baltic States, whose entry into the EU would be far more acceptable to Moscow than their entry into NATO. In addition to providing reassurance about the West's commitment to CEE in the face of an uncertain future in Russia, early enlargement would also diminish fears in CEE about German domination because accession would provide the region a voice within the same club.

Unfortunately, there is a growing temptation in Brussels and particularly in the European Parliament to seek ("an accountant's solution"[40])of late enlargement and partial membership to the millenial mission of integrating CEE into the West. Recent studies by the European Commission conclude that the extension of EU policies, most notably in the fields of agriculture and structural (development) funds, to the ten CEE countries which have applied for membership will cost the EU budget an extra ECU 38 billion ($50 billion) per year.

These studies are striking in that they focus on "worst-case scenarios" of costs resulting from enlargement rather than on strategies for limiting these costs, the counter-balancing benefits flowing from an enlarged single market, and the political imperatives of stabilizing Central and Eastern Europe. Although the average per capita income in CEE is considerably less than the average in the EU, the differential between the wealthiest candidates (Slovenia and the Czech Republic) and the poorest EU Member States (Greece, Portugal and Ireland) is much smaller. Moreover, the income differential between Greece, Spain and Portugal, on the one hand, and the rest of the Community, on the other, were nearly as great upon their accession. Although they may be "poor neighbors," they appear to be readier for EU membership than some current members when judged according to the Maastricht convergence criteria[41] or according to their willingness to respect EU collegiality and the rule of law.

Calculations by EU Budget Commissioner Liikanen indicate, moreover, that the costs of extending agricultural and structural aid programs to the CEE could be dramatically reduced if assistance were capped at a certain percentage of GDP and if disbursements were phased in over several years. The costs of enlargement, furthermore, are likely to be counterbalanced by trade creation and security benefits resulting from an expanded common market and a stable, prosperous east.

The important benefits of enlargement led the EU heads of state to make a political commitment in Madrid in December 1995 to start enlargement negotiations six months after the end of the IGC in 1997. Based on the questionnaire which it sent to the nine Central and Eastern European candidates for accession regarding their suitability for EU membership, the Commission may issue its formal *avis* by the end of 1996, thereby enabling formal negotiations to begin.[42] It is uncertain, however, how long the negotiations will continue and whether EU Member States will be deadlocked regarding when, how many, and in what sequence candidates should become members. Although it is possible that the most advanced candidates (the Czech Republic and Poland) could accede to the Union around the year 2000, it is more likely (particularly if Europe continues to suffer from slow growth and high unemployment) that formal negotiations with candidate members may be delayed until 1998-9 and that accession may begin only around 2002-3. In that case, the will of the CEE electorate to continue with economic reform could be severely undermined: advocates of the free market and democracy would no longer be able to urge continued sacrifice with the argument that rewards lie "around the corner."

Washington's support for early enlargement depends on the ability of the EU to take in new members while preserving its cohesiveness and ability to act as an effective partner of the United States.[43] Institutional reform is particularly pressing because the next rounds of enlargement, unlike previous ones, will bring countries into the EU with starkly heterogeneous political, economic and social characteristics. This point is, of course, well understood even at the highest levels of the Community's decision-making:

> enlarging the European Union from 15 to 20, 25 or even 30 countries in the future cannot happen without profound structural change in our institutions and in our decision-making procedures. Without appropriate reforms we will actually *weaken* the European Union -- *weaken* our ability to take decisive action and finally *weaken* security in Europe, which is in no-one's interest.[44]

American policy toward Europe would suffer a major setback if rapid enlargement without prior institutional reform causes the Union to disintegrate into a loose, free trade area.

Even though this scenario is unlikely, Washington might still be led to reassess its enthusiastic support for the EU if the IGC fails to adopt the reforms necessary to ensure that enlargement does not complicate and slow down internal decision-making or weaken the EU's ability to conduct international negotiations. The modest nature of the options presented by the Reflection Group tasked with framing issues for the Conference indicate that the reforms eventually adopted may not be sufficient to avoid these dangers. Although Washington has not formally expressed an opinion regarding the IGC, partly because this would be viewed as outside interference and partly because of the difficulty of reaching inter-agency consensus on so complex an issue, its perspective is clear: the Conference should seek to define rules which provide just enough flexibility to accommodate diversity without jeopardizing the Union's common structure, rules and objectives.

The construction of a Europe 'a la carte' in which Member States have complete freedom of choice about the core obligations which they are prepared to assume under the Union, or the construction of a Europe of loose 'variable geometry' in which Member States may 'opt-out' of Union policy, could eventually cause the erosion of the single market.[45] Once Member States can 'opt-out' of EU single market legislation, they may similarly refuse to be bound by the Union's competence to conduct international negotiations relating to the same areas. If the EU were to lose its ability to speak for all its members in such negotiations, its attractiveness to the United States would decline significantly.[46]

Washington might also reexamine its support for EU enlargement if there were a threat that the new members might immediately adopt Western Europe's overly rigid and expensive welfare and labor legislation as part of the EU's *acquis communautaire*. Such adoption would risk undermining the competitiveness of the new members, thereby preventing them from achieving the high growth rates necessary to close the gap between them and their EU partners. Prisoners of the EU's social legislation and perhaps a monetary regime restricting currency devaluation, the new members could find themselves locked into a permanent state of economic inferiority. This may have already been the experience of Spain, Portugal and, in particular, Greece which have failed to grow rapidly enough over the last decade to attain average EU income levels. If the new members fail to achieve growth rates which are significantly higher than those in Western Europe, popular disenchantment with market economics, and perhaps even with democracy, may ensue.

Washington's support for EU enlargement is also conditioned on the view that the entry of new EU members as full members of the WEU should be synchronized, although not necessarily simultaneous, with their entry into NATO. Full membership in the WEU *before* membership in NATO would give rise to a "back-door security guarantee" by NATO based on Article V of the North Atlantic Treaty. According to some observers in the Administration, this risk would be particularly acute if a Baltic State were to be a full WEU member and were attacked by Russia. In such a case, it would be automatically entitled to military assistance from its fellow WEU members under the terms of the WEU Treaty. If these members were also NATO members and were attacked in turn, the United States would find itself bound to defend a state to which it had not extended guarantees under the NATO Treaty.

In addition to projecting stability to CEE, the EU has also projected stability to those parts of the former Soviet bloc for which membership in the EU is not a viable option or is not, in the case of the Baltic States, likely in the short term. The EU's strategy has consisted of agreements establishing or envisaging free trade, technical assistance for market reforms, financial assistance and political dialogue. Free trade agreements with the Baltic States were signed at the beginning of 1995 and have been replaced with Association ("Europe") Agreements modelled on those with Central and Eastern Europe. Whereas the EU's Partnership and Cooperation Agreement with Russia only envisages free trade as a long term goal, it encourages political dialogue, increased trade and support for economic reform, particularly in market liberalization and the adoption of competition rules. The agreement makes a contribution as important as any other, including the Partnership for Peace (PFP), in ensuring that Russia develops a peaceful and democratic orientation.

Brussels appears to share Washington's fear of a resurgence of aggressive nationalism in Russia and the desire to promote the economic and political stability of Belarus, Moldova and, in particular, Ukraine so that they may serve as buffer states for Europe. The EU has signed Partnership and Cooperation Agreements with all three and has joined the United States in contributing to IMF-sponsored balance of payments assistance to them. In addition, the EU has joined the US in providing financial and technical assistance for the closure of Chernobyl. In the case of the former Central Asian republics of the Soviet Union, the EU has focussed on providing financial and technical assistance through its TACIS program.

The EU as ally in stabilizing the Third World

In addition to projecting stability eastwards, the EU is a valued ally of Washington in stabilizing the Third World. With the end of the Cold War, the tendency of Europe and the United States to consider their security needs in predominantly military terms has receded. Militant Islamic fundamentalism, high population growth rates and poor economic performance in Northern Africa and the Middle East are among the principal security threats to Europe and the United States today because of the economic and political upheaval and emigration which they may trigger. Washington recognizes that the EU plays a key role in the transatlantic objective of stabilizing these regions with a mixture of trade, aid and technical assistance for free market reforms.

The Commission is responsible for distributing 15 per cent of EU Member States' total foreign aid (including development and humanitarian aid) and half of their humanitarian aid. The EU's 1996 budget calls for ECU 850 million for food aid, with another ECU 730 million devoted to development aid, to be distributed by the European Community Humanitarian Aid Office (ECHO).

Although the United States is the second largest donor after the European Union,[47] its foreign aid is the lowest of any official donor when expressed as a percentage of GDP and is heavily concentrated in just two countries -- Israel and Egypt. Budgetary pressures and the turn toward unilateralism and isolationism, partly in reaction to the traumatic experience of the US with its failed humanitarian mission to Somalia, will reduce US foreign aid even further. As a result, Washington will increasingly turn to the EU to help cope with humanitarian crises in the Third World and to achieve common objectives there -- the promotion of democracy, regional stability and economic prosperity.

There is growing appreciation in Washington of the fact that the United States cannot achieve these objectives in Africa without the assistance of the EU. In addition to its food and development aid, the EU supported the

39

transition to democracy in South Africa by providing the bulk of election observers and will continue to give aid for infrastructure development and education (ECU 125 million in 1996). It has also played a critical part in humanitarian missions to relieve the suffering in Rwanda and Burundi.

Long-term stability in Africa depends as much on the access to Western markets as on the West's provision of humanitarian assistance. Here, too, the EU has and will continue to play an important role. Unfortunately, narrow concerns under US trade laws have occasionally subsumed Washington's broader political interests in supporting EU initiatives in Africa. While recognizing the importance of maintaining a market for the raw materials of the world's poorest countries, Washington has often criticized the preferential policies which the EU implements to support this objective. Two objects of such criticism have been the Lomé Convention and the EU's banana regime.[48]

The 1989 Lomé IV Convention will keep the European market open until the turn of the century to the exports of the poorest African countries, mostly former European colonies, by exempting them from customs duties.[49] USTR has traditionally opposed the Convention because it contains discriminatory preferences which contravene GATT principles of free trade. In early 1995 the EU renewed its GATT waiver for the Convention. Even without the waiver, however, it is arguable that the political importance of the Convention should, from the perspective of the United States, outweigh its incompatibility with the GATT. Many of the African, Caribbean and Pacific (ACP) countries benefiting from preferences under Lomé rely on exports of a few agricultural products or raw materials for their livelihood. Eliminating such preferences would lead to reduced export earnings, higher indebtedness, greater poverty and social unrest.

USTR has also conducted a lengthy campaign against the EU's banana marketing regime which grants preferential market access to ACP banana exporters, despite the fact that the regime only injures the US in an indirect and inconsequential manner: although the US does not export bananas (and therefore does not have jobs at stake in the sector), one US multinational -- Chiquita Brands -- claims that its profits, and US shareholders, suffer because of European quotas. Dole and Del Monte, Chiquita's main US competitors, are not complaining about the EU's regime because they have larger investments in the favored Caribbean area than in Central and Latin America.[50]

Senator Bob Dole, who has long been supported and financed by Carl Lindner, the president of Chiquita Brands, opposed the EU regime vigorously on Capitol Hill during 1993-5. Partly as a result of Congressional pressure, USTR threatened to take action under Section 301 of the 1974 Trade Act[51] against the EU for implementing the discriminatory regime and against Colombia and Costa Rica for having signed so-called "Framework Agreements" (quota deals) settling their disputes with the EU. Although USTR finally dropped its threat of trade sanctions against Colombia and Costa Rica once Dole and Chiquita were given a share of their quotas, it is simultaneously pursuing its Section 301 case against the EU banana regime and prosecuting a second complaint (supported by Ecuador, Guatemala, Honduras, Panama and Mexico) with the WTO.

The logic behind USTR's threat to take action against the EU under Section 301 is that US trade laws not only exist to protect American jobs, but also the market share and profits of American companies abroad and, perhaps, even the value of shares held in these companies by American investors. The USTR is naturally obliged to enforce US trade laws, including Section 301, and its interpretations of the statutes may be legally defensible.[52] But the scale of US interests at stake hardly seems to justify making the EU Banana Regulation a major target of US trade policy. Moreover, it is open to question whether attacking the EU for granting preferential access to ACP banana exports at a time of declining US foreign and development aid is consistent with the overriding US objective of promoting economic growth and political stability in the Third World.

Of course, the Regulation's discrimination against the "dollar bananas" of Central and Latin America injures the region's economic and political stability. That is precisely why Colombia and Costa Rica sought, after having failed to gain any material relief from two GATT panels ruling that the Regulation contravenes several key GATT rules, to safeguard their major banana exporting industries by concluding Framework Agreements increasing EU quotas and reducing EU tariffs for "dollar bananas." By threatening these countries with action under Section 301, rather than seeking to resolve the dispute with the EU through the WTO's binding dispute settlement procedures, the USTR regrettably gave primacy to the narrow interest of protecting the profits of a single US company over wider US interests to enhance the effectiveness of the WTO and over Central and Latin American efforts to safeguard a critical export industry.

As in Africa, the EU is playing a critical role in promoting regional development and stability on the Southern rim of the Mediterranean by means of trade and aid. By improving the climate for investment, enhancing the competitiveness of local industries and creating jobs, the EU is advancing the joint US-EU objective of relieving economic crises, averting political upheavals and mass migration.

The Euro-Mediterranean Conference of foreign ministers in Barcelona on 27-28 November 1995 confirmed a regional aid package of $6 billion over the next five years for many of the countries bordering on the Mediterranean. The EU's 1996 budget earmarks ECU 900 million to North

41

African and Middle Eastern states in the Mediterranean. Its trading relations with the region are equally significant: the EU absorbs more than 70 per cent of the Maghreb's exports and provides almost 65 per cent of its imports. Moreover, the EU has signed association agreements with Tunisia and Morocco which provide for gradual establishment of free trade and closer political cooperation and is soon to conclude similar agreements with Egypt, Jordan and Lebanon. Its agreement with Israel expands the scope of the 1975 Free Trade Agreement by including services, open bidding for public procurement contracts and greater cooperation on research and development.

These agreements, analogous to existing "Europe Agreements" with east Europeans on everything except eventual EU membership, represent a significant step toward the goal of establishing between now and 2010 a "Euro-Med" free-trade zone between the EU and a dozen Northern African and Middle East countries bordering the Mediterranean Sea. American exporters may be marginally disadvantaged by these arrangements; but the net effect of lost export opportunities in this market, which is of limited importance for the United States, will likely be compensated by the improvement in the region's political and economic stability.

The EU has also played an important role in promoting the Middle East peace process through the Euro-Arab dialogue, hosting the 1991 Madrid Conference which opened direct talks between Israel and its Arab neighbors, and providing considerable financial assistance. According to the World Bank, the EU has supplied 37 per cent of all aid to the Middle East since 1993. It is widely recognized, including by the parties in the region, that Washington's diplomatic engagement, prestige, and military power have been critical in keeping the negotiations on track. But the strict budgetary constraints that the US Congress is imposing on the conduct of American foreign policy mean that the Clinton Administration cannot provide all the financial and material means to ensure the peace.

The EU has pledged a five-year aid package of $560 million in grants and loans, slightly more than the US, for infrastructure projects, housing and job creation programs in agriculture, tourism and small scale industry in Gaza and the West Bank. The industrial free trade agreements which the EU has concluded with these territories, and the prospect of enhanced access to Europe's agricultural market, have also contributed to their economic viability. Moreover, the EU supervised the Palestinian elections, as well as providing half of the 700 election monitors, equipped the territory's police force and provided roughly $250 million in humanitarian aid for the period 1994-98. These measures may not have been as high profile or as tangibly beneficial as Secretary of State Warren Christopher's shuttle diplomacy in the region or US sponsorship of talks between Israel and its Arab neighbors; but they were critical nonetheless.

42

The modest attention given by the international media to the EU's role in the Middle East has frequently prompted European governments to complain that they write the checks while the United States garners the credit. Although the complaint is partly justified, the reason for this state of affairs lies rather more in the failure of the EU to assume a unified political role in the region and to "market" its significant economic role more effectively rather than in an effort by American administrations to monopolize the limelight. The main reasons for the EU's low political profile in the region include France's efforts to retain its traditionally strong diplomatic presence, the deep cleavages of opinion within the EU regarding the Arab-Israeli conflict which often result in "lowest common denominator" policies, and the realization on the part of all parties to the conflict that the United States is the only country with sufficient diplomatic influence and military power to play the role of mediator.

On the eastern rim of the Mediterranean, the EU has also advanced US objectives regarding the reinforcement of Turkey's Western orientation and the settlement of the Cyprus conflict. It brokered a deal whereby Greece lifted its long-standing veto on an EU customs union with Turkey in exchange for a pledge by the EU to start accession negotiations for the entire island six months after the conclusion of the Inter-Governmental Conference. The prospect of EU accession is one of the most important factors promoting inter-communal dialogue in Cyprus and strengthening human rights and democracy in Turkey.

Naturally, the convergence of US and EU interests in the Middle East is not absolute: the lifting of the EU's arms embargo on Syria, the EU's "critical dialogue" with Iran (despite the latter's continued support for international terrorism and refusal to lift its death sentence against British author Salman Rushdie) and the EU's tepid support for the Middle East Development Bank and the Korean Energy Development Organization (KEDO)[53] are among the most serious irritants in the political relations between Brussels and Washington. From the perspective of th`e United Slegal tests of Iraq's liability in a manner which will provide to a maximum number of deserving claimants the maximum compensation consistent severely limited financial resources.tates, these policies reflect the particular interests of certain Member States and one of the EU's abiding weaknesses -- the vulnerability of its foreign policy process to being hijacked by its most vocal actors.

The EU as ally in addressing global challenges

One of the central reasons why the Clinton Administration has been a strong supporter of European integration is that the EU is increasingly developing into a global partner of the United States on a broad range of transnational

43

problems which are beyond the powers of individual countries to resolve single-handedly: international trafficking in drugs and nuclear materials, environmental crises (especially climate change, air and water pollution, desertification, the protection of endangered species and the depletion of marine resources), famine, disease, migration and the slide of the Third World toward greater poverty and political instability. Moreover, despite high growth rates in East Asia, the United States and the EU remain the key actors in the international trading regime. The success of past efforts to liberalize and expand world trade, including the Uruguay Round, has been due to compromises reached between Washington and Brussels. Today, the success of the WTO, the accession of China and Russia, and the global expansion of free trade still depend on a close partnership between them.

Notes

1   "Cool Winds From the White House," *The Economist*, 27 March 1993, p. 36.
2   John Peterson, "Clinton and America in the Clinton Era," *Journal of Common Market Studies*, volume 32, no. 3, September 1994, p. 417.
3   In distinction to the postwar period, the continuing threat of fragmentation arises today in the context of strong popular attachment to Europe's regions rather than its nation states, as indicated by the increasingly vigorous assertion of regional autonomy in Belgium, Italy and Spain. Although the progressive pooling of sovereignty within the EU at the supranational level has held these fissiparous tendencies in check, it may paradoxically have contributed to the rise in regional power by promoting the decomposition of the nation state.
4   As quoted in David Marsh, "EMU Strain Begins to Show," *The Financial Times*, 17 January 1995.
5   Alberta Sbragia, "Transatlantic Relations: An Evolving Mosaic," Paper presented to a conference in Brussels on Policy-Making and Decision-Making in Transatlantic Relations, 3-4 May 1996, p. 30.
6   The Commission has declared that it will take Member States that sign or implement bilateral "open skies" agreements with the United States to the Court of Justice. In late June 1996, EU transport ministers granted the European Commission a two-stage mandate to

begin negotiations with Washington for a gradual liberalization of the transatlantic air market. According to this mandate, the first stage of the negotiations are to cover regulatory issues, including competition, state aid, restrictions on foreign ownership of air companies, airport slot allocation, computerized reservation systems and flight code sharing. Depending on the success of these negotiations, the Council may decide to instruct the European Commission to engage in second-stage negotiations on reciprocal market access and mutual granting of air traffic rights. At the time this book went to press, it was uncertain, however, whether the United States would accept entering into first-stage negotiations separately from the second stage in which it has greater interest.

7   "A Ghost At the Feast," *The Economist*, 19 February 1994, p. 20. Emphasis added.

8   There is no indication that a decrease in the "democratic deficit" through greater influence of the European Parliament would damage the interests of the United States. The Parliament's support for the Commission's creation of the single market indicates that it is unlikely to act as a protectionist and antiliberal force. See Miles Kahler, *Regional Futures and Transatlantic Economic Relations*, Council on Foreign Relations Press, 1995, p. 33. Nor is there any indication that the Clinton Administration has formulated a view regarding the institutional balance between Community institutions which it would like to emerge from the IGC.

9   More specifically, enlargement hastens the transfer of political leadership of the Union from France to Germany. This is likely to be advantageous to the United States, as it has greater interests in common with Bonn than with Paris.

10   Opinion 1/94 of the Court of Justice, 15 November 1994. [1994] ECR I-5267. The Court found that, whereas the supply of services implying a movement of persons or an establishment within the EU falls within the concurrent competence of the EU and its Member States, those services which do not do so fall within the ambit of the common commercial policy and therefore within the exclusive competence of the Community. According to the Court, although the Community shares competence with the Member States with regard to the agreement on Trade-Related Aspects of Intellectual Property, the Community acquires exclusive competence if it has taken internal harmonization measures. It is estimated that roughly

30 per cent of all trade between the US and the EU will be in services by the end of the century.

11 These criteria consist of the following financial targets which Member States must fulfill in order to be part of the single currency: (1) an average rate of inflation which does not exceed by more than 1.5 per cent the average of the three best performing Member States; (2) the avoidance of an excessive government budgetary deficit, defined as an annual budget deficit of less than 3 per cent of GDP and an overall public debt ratio not exceeding 60 per cent of GDP; (3) a currency which has been within the normal fluctuation margins of the Exchange Rate Mechanism of the European Monetary System without severe tensions for a period of time; and (4) an average long-term interest rate does not exceed by more than two per cent the average interest rates in the three best performing states in terms of price stability.

12 The decline of the dollar's role as a reserve currency will result in a small loss of "seignorage income" for the United States -- the purchasing power gained from non-interest bearing reserve dollars held by foreign central banks. See Randall Henning, "Europe's Monetary Union and the United States," *Foreign Policy*, Spring 1996.

13 *Ibid.*

14 In 1992 the US Treasury expressed concern that the Maastricht Treaty's convergence criteria would slow down economic growth in Europe and worldwide. Martin Feldstein, former Chairman of the Council of Economic Advisers, has argued that the economic disadvantages for Europe of a single currency outweigh the political advantages. See "The Case Against EMU," *The Economist*, 13 June 1992, pp. 19-22.

15 According to Under-Secretary of State Joan Spero, "We are supportive of their efforts to create EMU, but at the same time, we do not want EMU to be developed at the expense of a massive slowdown in the European economy." See Tim Jones, "US in Two Minds Over Euro," *European Voice*, 11-17 July 1996. Joseph Stiglitz, chairman of the Council of Economic Advisers, and Lawrence Summers, Deputy Secretary of the Treasury, allegedly voiced similar concerns during the G-7 conference of finance and employment ministers in April 1996.

16   US Department of State, "Charting a Transatlantic Agenda for the 21st Century," Speech by Secretary of State Warren Christopher, 2 June 1995 in Madrid.

17   Timothy Garten Ash, "Bosnia in Our Future," *New York Review of Books*, 21 December 1995.

18   As outgoing US Assistant Secretary of State, Richard Holbrooke, told the press during the crisis: "While President Clinton was on the phone with Athens and Ankara, the Europeans were literally sleeping through the night." See "US Polices Aegean 'While EU Sleeps,'" *The Financial Times*, 9 February 1996.

19   Speech Before the European Institute, 9 May 1995, as reproduced in "The United States and the 1996 Inter-Governmental Conference," ed. Peter Rashish, The European Institute (1995).

20   The Commission represents the Community in the Organization for Economic Cooperation and Development, the Organization for Security and Cooperation in Europe (OSCE) and the World Intellectual Property Organization. Former Commission President Jacques Delors successfully fought to be a full-fledged delegate to the Conference on Security and Cooperation in Europe (CSCE), the predecessor to the OSCE, and was one of the 35 signatories to its Charter of Paris on 21 November 1990. The European Commission President has participated in the world economic summit meetings of the G-7 heads of state and government since the 1980 summit in Venice. At the world economic summit meeting in Tokyo in 1986, however, Secretary of the Treasury James Baker III blocked Delors' bid to gain a seat for the Commission at the table during meetings of G-7 finance ministers and central bankers. See Axel Krause, *Inside the New Europe*, Harper Collins 1991, p. 291.

21   In July 1996, for example, France and Britain applied for membership in the Association of South East Asian Nations (ASEAN) Regional Forum, a caucus for debating security issues in the region, even though the EU was already a member. The Commission criticized the move as indicating a lack of trust by Paris and London in the ability of the EU to represent their interests. See James Kynge, "EU Angry at UK, France On Asean Move," *The Financial Times*, 24 July 1996.

22   Mark Nelson and G. John Ikenberry, *Atlantic Frontiers: A New Agenda for US-EC Relations*, Carnegie Endowment for International Peace 1993, pp. 19-20, as quoted in Miles Kahler,

Regional Futures and Transatlantic Economic Relations, Council on Foreign Relations Press 1995, p. 26.

23   The Delegation's ability to represent the EU on trade issues in Washington is particularly significant when the Member States are united in opposition to the United States during trade disputes. The transatlantic disputes regarding the Helms-Burton Act and the D'Amato Bill, imposing US law extraterritorially to sanction companies and persons who "traffic" in property confiscated by the Castro regime or who invest in the oil and gas sectors in Iran and Libya, respectively, are good cases in point. See Chapter 8.

24   Speech before the European Institute, 12 May 1994, as reproduced in "The United States and the 1996 Inter-Governmental Conference," ed. Peter Rashish, The European Institute (1995).

25   Edward Mortimer, "Eurostructures Under One Roof," *The Financial Times*, 3 May 1995.

26   That view has been echoed in the Commission's Opinion on "Reinforcing Political Union and Preparing for Enlargement" of 28 February 1996, COM(96)90 final: "...the Common Foreign and Security Policy cannot develop without real political resolve on the part of the Member States, together with clearly-defined objectives." At point 28. The opinion also notes that "[a] genuine European identity in the security and defense field is indispensable. It requires clear political will on the part of Member States." At point 34.

27   According to a Eurobarometer poll, few Europeans consider themselves as purely European. Although at most a tenth of Belgians and Luxembourgers see themselves "in the near future" as purely European, half of the British, Portuguese and Greeks, and a third of the Germans, Spanish and Dutch see themselves in purely national terms. "More-or-less European Union," *The Economist*, 26 August 1995, p. 46.

28   Article J.4(2). Belgium, France, Greece, Germany, Italy, Luxembourg, the Netherlands, Portugal, Spain and the United Kingdom are full members of the WEU. Austria, Denmark, Finland, Ireland and Sweden hold observer status because of their traditional neutrality. Iceland, Norway and Turkey are associate members.

29   "The Defence of Europe: It Can't Be Done Alone," *The Economist*, 25 February 1995, p. 19.

30   The forces which EU Member States have earmarked to support WEU operations are Eurocorps (an army force based in Strasbourg

comprising troops from Belgium, France, Germany, Luxembourg and Spain), Eurofor (a rapid reaction force headquartered in Florence and composed of 12,000 infantry with light artillery from France, Italy, Portugal and Spain), Euromarfor (a naval force led by a French aircraft carrier and composed of French, Italian, Portuguese and Spanish troops), and the UK-Netherlands Amphibious Task Force (a roughly 5,000 troop British marine force and several Dutch battalions with hovercraft and amphibious ships, accompanied by naval escorts).

31   "Commission Calls for EU's Rules to Cover Arms," *The Wall Street Journal*, 27-28 January 1996.

32   From 1988 to 1992 EU members imported almost $18 billion in conventional arms from the United States and exported less than $1 billion to the US. While three quarters of arms imports came from the United States during that period, intra-European trade amounted to less than 4 per cent of total procurement of such arms. "EU Promotes Own Weapons," *International Herald Tribune*, 26 January 1996.

33   It is too early to judge whether the agreement on Combined Joint Task Forces reached during the NATO ministerial meeting in Berlin in early June 1996 will significantly advance the WEU's capabilities. Although the agreement is important because it further recognizes Europe's aspirations to assume greater responsibility, and independence, in ensuring its own security, the practical consequences may be rather more limited in the short term. Under the Berlin agreement, the WEU would be able to "borrow" NATO assets for missions in which the United States chooses not to participate, but only under three conditions imposed by Washington: "the United States approves of the mission; the overall responsible commander for NATO assets remains the (American) Supreme Allied Commander; and the forces involved are all NATO-approved and follow NATO procedures." See Philip Gordon, "'European-ization' of NATO: A Convenient Myth," *International Herald Tribune*, 7 June 1996.

34   Quoted in "The Politics of Peace," *The Economist*, 1 April 1995, p. 17.

35   US Department of State, "Charting a Transatlantic Agenda for the 21st Century," Speech by Secretary of State Warren Christopher in Madrid on 2 June 1995.

36   Some officials involved in this EU-CEE "structural dialogue" lament that these meetings have degenerated into set pieces featuring the exchange of prepared speaches which evoke "a degree of boredom exceptional even by the generous standards of international diplomacy." Thomas Klau, "Tackling the Structural Monologue," *European Voice*, 22-28 February 1996, p. 11. Although there is clearly no substitute to the meaningful dialogue which would occur in the context of accession negotiations, these meetings nonetheless serve the useful purpose of bringing high-level EU and CEE leaders together regularly, keeping pressure on the EU to commit to an early start to such negotiations, and focussing the minds of CEE leaders on the prerequisites to accession.

37   The picture is significantly different with regard to investment. US investors have accounted for roughly 40 per cent of foreign direct investment in CEE, compared to slightly over 40 per cent for investors from the 12 EU Member States combined. Enlargement to Austria, Finland and Sweden has probably increased the share for the EU.

38   At the end of 1991, half of Poland's exports to the EC were subject to some kind of trade restraint. "Business in Eastern Europe," Supplement to *The Economist*, 21 September 1991, p. 9. In early 1993, 40% of Polish, Hungarian and Czech exports to the EU were still subject to trade restraints. "The Old World's New World," Supplement to *The Economist*, 13 March 1993, p. 20.

39   Lionel Barber, "Brussels Keeps Shut the Gates to the East," *The Financial Times*, 16 November 1995, p. 17.

40   David Lawday, "The Return of the Habsburgs," Special Supplement to *The Economist*, 18 November 1995, p. 7.

41   See "The Old World's New World," Special Supplement to *The Economist*, 13 March 1993, p. 21.

42   The *avis* will be based on whether the applicants meet the conditions for accession: (1) stability of institutions guaranteeing democracy, the rule of law, human rights, and respect for and protection of minorities; (2) the existence of a functioning market economy; (3) capacity to cope with competitive pressure and market forces within the Union; and (4) ability to take on the obligations of membership including adherence to the aims of political, Economic and Monetary Union.

43   As Miles Kahler of the Council on Foreign Relations has aptly put it, the United States seeks from the EU "clarity of competence, ability to coordinate internally, and reasonable efficiency in reaching a common position." Miles Kahler, *Regional Futures and Transatlantic Economic Relations*, Council on Foreign Relations Press 1995, p. 28.

44   Speech by European Commission President Jacques Santer before the European Institute, 15 June 1995.

45   This is in contrast to a "multi-speed" Europe in which there is a "hard core" of Member States pursuing integration more quickly than others, but in which all Member States share the same ultimate objectives.

46   Lionel Barber, "Fresh Meat from Europe's Stable," *The Financial Times*, 8 December 1994.

47   In 1994 the United States spent approximately $1.6 billion on humanitarian assistance.

47   Council Regulation (EEC) No. 404/93 of 13 February 1993 on the common organisation of the market in bananas, O.J. 1993, L47/1.

49   On 4 November 1995 the EU agreed to extend trade privileges and roughly $18 billion in aid to the 70 African, Caribbean and Pacific members of Lomé through the year 2000.

50   Whereas the market share of Dole and Del Monte in the EU banana market rose from 11 per cent to 15 per cent and from 7.5 per cent to 8 per cent between 1991 to 1994, respectively, the market share of Chiquita dropped from 25 per cent to 18.5 per cent during the same time period.

51   19 USC 2411.

52   Section 301(a)(1)(B)(ii) provides that the Trade Representative shall take action under the section if "an act, policy or practice of a foreign country...is unjustifiable and burdens or restricts United States commerce." Although the Banana Regulation may be unjustifiable, it is uncertain whether it burdens or restricts US commerce (as opposed to US interests). Section 301(b) requires the Trade Representative to "take all appropriate and feasible action" to obtain the elimination of any act, policy or practice which is "unreasonable or discriminatory and burdens or restricts United States commerce..." provided that action by the United States is appropriate. It is open to question whether the Regulation is "unreasonable," as defined in Section 301(d)(3)(B)(i)(IV), in that it

denies fair and equitable market opportunities for US goods in a foreign market. The 'dollar bananas' cultivated in Central and Latin America and the Caribbean by US multinationals are arguably Costa Rican, Colombian, Ecuadorian, Guatemalan or Honduran bananas; the fact that they are cultivated by US multinationals may not be sufficient to make them "US goods." Although the Banana Regulation is certainly discriminatory, it is unclear whether the Regulation burdens or restricts US commerce. Even if the Regulation were disriminatory and burdens or restricts US commerce, it is far from clear whether, in light of overall US political and strategic interests and of other unfair trade practices around the world which require redress, action by the United States against the Regulation would be appropriate.

53   KEDO is designed to dismantle North Korea's nuclear weapons program and prevent its withdrawal from the Nuclear Non-Proliferation Treaty by offering it a variety of political and economic benefits, including aid and technical assistance in developing alternative energy sources. After many months of delay, the European Union finally approved a contribution of ECU 5 million to KEDO on 5 March 1996. This is in addition to individual contributions by France, Germany, Italy, the Netherlands and the United Kingdom. The European Commission has sought to increase the EU contribution to ECU 15 million per year to match US contributions in order to ensure that EU industries are able to participate fully in KEDO's commercial opportunities.

Part Two
The New Transatlantic Agenda

5 The three Berlin working groups

As described in Chapter 3, three working groups were launched at the US-EU summit in July 1994 in Berlin. These groups were primarily the creation of Bernhard Zepter, assistant to President Delors, Joachim Bitterlich, National Security Adviser to Chancellor Kohl, and Under-Secretary for Political Affairs Peter Tarnoff. In order to avoid creating another layer of bureaucracy and to assuage French concerns about Washington's insinuation into EU policy making, the Commission, Germany (which was holding the EU presidency in rotation) and the United States agreed that the working groups would have the limited mandate of preparing the agenda for the next US-EU Summit in Washington, at which time they would disband. Some EU Member States had urged that the full Troika (Germany, France and Greece) represent the EU in the working groups; the Commission had lobbied in favor of holding the meetings in a trilateral format because it would diminish the representation of the Member States and thereby enhance its ability to act as the EU's foreign policy voice. The Commission's point of view prevailed, partly because the troika mechanism had been conceived as a device to ensure continuity for permanent arrangements and was, therefore, unsuited to working groups of limited duration.

The leaders agreed that the groups would focus on three areas: international crime, including drug trafficking, nuclear smuggling and money laundering; Common Foreign and Security Policy, particularly the means of improving coordination on humanitarian assistance to the Third World; and Central and Eastern Europe, particularly the means of improving coordination in technical assistance programs for market reform.

The working group on international crime

The working group on international crime was formed at the insistence of Chancellor Kohl, who wished to forge a transatlantic response to a serious threat emerging along Germany's eastern frontier: smuggling of plutonium, drug trafficking, money laundering and illegal immigration.

Nuclear-related smuggling presented, perhaps, the most serious risk: in 1994 alone, there were three seizures in Germany of significant amounts of weapons-grade material. The disintegration of the Soviet empire had led to a sharp reduction in the Russian military budget and a decline in living standards for scientists at research facilities and employees at nuclear installations; their access to fissionable materials and sensitive nuclear technology made them prime targets for corruption by terrorists groups and the mafia. Moreover, Moscow's weakening grip over Russian economic and political life, combined with the sudden porousness of Central and Eastern European frontiers, had allowed local mafia, most notably in Chechnya, to forge relationships with international crime syndicates.

The European Commission supported Germany's request for a working group on international crime, primarily as a back-door way of acquiring competences which had been granted to the Council under the "Third Pillar" of the Maastricht Treaty. EU Member States have considered that "Home and Justice Affairs," consisting of police powers and law enforcement, involved sensitive issues of sovereignty and should therefore be dealt by means of inter-governmental, rather than communitarian, decision-making. But the Commission has argued that these issues also impact upon the single market and have trans-frontier consequences which can only be managed with effectively at a supranational level. It has been supported in this view by the United States: from Washington's perspective, conducting a dialogue with a single European interlocutor on international crime is preferable to doing so with fifteen. That view is reflected in Washington's enthusiasm for EUROPOL, the nascent European police force, despite full knowledge of its likely limitations. By engaging the EU on 'third pillar' issues in one of the Berlin working groups, moreover, the United States hoped to help the EU overcome its institutional weakness and develop into an effective interlocutor.

The working group on international crime ran into trouble almost immediately because several Member States suspected it to be part of a

Commission 'plot' to bring "home and justice affairs" within the Community's competence in contradiction to the Maastricht Treaty's clear provisions that such affairs should be handled inter-governmentally. In addition, the French Government (Interior Minister Charles Pasqua in particular) was resolutely opposed to conducting exchanges of sensitive information regarding international crime, and terrorism in particular, with the United States. France had vigorously opposed, for example, an agreement between the Commission and the Drug Enforcement Agency on sharing information about precursor chemical diversions.

The failure of the working group also reflected the weakness of Third Pillar cooperation and, specifically, the inability of the EU Member States to agree on the nature of information to be exchanged among themselves. Finally, its failure was also due to a bureaucratic tug-of-war between the coordinators for Third Pillar issues in the Council and Commission secretariats and between the EU and the interior ministries of its Member States.

As a result, initiatives of the US Department of Justice, Federal Bureau of Investigation (FBI) and the Drug Enforcement Agency -- calling for the establishment of a joint data bank on Russian organized crime, a clearinghouse to coordinate drug and law enforcement training programs in third countries and an agreement on information sharing on chemical precursors -- were met with the refrain that intra-European coordination on Third Pillar issues was still in its infancy and that the United States needed to be patient.

The working group on Common Foreign and Security Policy

The senior US representative on the CFSP working group, Principal Deputy Assistant Secretary of State John Kornblum, sought to focus the group's work on developing mechanisms for real-time operational interaction between Washington and Brussels. This focus reflected the State Department's long-standing frustration of not knowing whether to work principally with the EU Presidency or Commission during a crisis -- such as Iraq's invasion of Kuwait, the conflict in Bosnia or the civil war in Rwanda. The group acknowledged the need for improved consultations between US and EU diplomatic missions in the Third World in order to predict political crises and prepare a coordinated evacuation of nationals, to provide emergency food and medical aid more quickly and in a more coordinated manner to areas afflicted by natural disasters, and to respond more effectively to the outbreak of hostilities (as in Bosnia) or political crises such as coups. But the group was unable to agree on the mechanisms for such consultation.

The group discussed how to give greater structure to the irregular pattern of consultations between the heads of mission of the EU troika and US ambassadors in unstable regions of Africa, Latin America and the Middle East. The US proposed that the EU should designate a single "lead" EU embassy in each region for the purpose of facilitating US-EU contacts and coordination on the ground. The idea was not pursued, however, partly because it was feared that this would be seen as reinforcing the special role played by certain European countries in their former colonies. The group also considered the promotion of joint démarches on human rights by the missions of the US and the European Commission and EU presidency country, representing the 15 Member States, in third countries -- such as Burma and Haiti -- where their approaches were complementary.

The CFSP working group failed to live up to its aspirations. This was due in part to reticence in several Member States to granting the Commission a role in the definition and implementation of CFSP when the Council was competent under the Maastricht Treaty's "Second Pillar." France did not want to grant Washington any say in the development of Europe's nascent foreign policy because it feared that that would diminish its own preeminence as Europe's spokesman. The group also suffered from a problem similar to that afflicting the group on international crime: transatlantic cooperation could not advance as long as intra-EU cooperation remained underdeveloped. The "Second Pillar" of the Maastricht Treaty dealing with CFSP had provided for cumbersome decision-making procedures and a complex division of competences among the EU institutions which prevented the EU from acting rapidly or coherently. Finally, the group suffered from the German Presidency's fixation on procedure which resulted in "non-papers" focussing nearly exclusively on mechanisms for cooperation -- the frequency and timing of meetings, the representation required at these meetings and the chain of authority between various levels of consultation -- rather than on practical areas of cooperation.

The working group on Central and Eastern Europe

One of the original objectives of the working group on Central and Eastern Europe was to coordinate US and EU foreign aid and technical assistance programs in the region. But this coordination function was already being carried out between Deputy Director General for External Economic Relations Robert Verrue of the European Commission, on the one hand, and

Coordinator for Assistance Ralph Johnson at the State Department and Senior Director for Central Europe Ambassador Richard Schifter at the National Security Council, on the other. The group considered several valuable ideas for initiatives in the fields of politics, economics and the environment. It agreed that the United States and the European Union could more effectively promote their shared objective of consolidating political and economic reform in the region by coordinating positions in international financial institutions, such as the World Bank, International Monetary Fund and European Bank for Reconstruction and Development; supporting regional efforts at economic integration and political cooperation; and by making complementary démarches to specific countries, such as Hungary about the need for fiscal responsibility and Slovakia about the dangers of backsliding on democracy.

The group also lent support to two regional centers in Budapest for law enforcement and the environment. It highlighted the need jointly to support training programs in Western crime prevention and investigation, due process and human rights for law enforcement officers from Central and Eastern Europe. The EU agreed that the International Law Enforcement Academy, established by the FBI in Budapest in 1991, would be an appropriate platform for this exercise. The group also examined how to strengthen the Regional Environmental Center established in Budapest upon the initiative of the United States and jointly funded by it along with the EU and Japan. Several transboundary air and water cleanup projects were considered.

The working group on Central and Eastern Europe identified areas of potential cooperation, but was unable to make concrete recommendations to the June 1995 summit in Washington. One reason for this may have been the Commission's latent suspicion of US proposals for common initiatives in the region as being secretly intended to give Washington a more prominent role while leaving the EU to bear the bulk of the cost. This had already been a familiar complaint concerning the Middle East: Washington was getting all the credit for the peace process despite the EU's sponsorship of the Madrid Conference and significant financial support for regional economic reconstruction.

The working group shied away from making proposals for significant initiatives. In February 1994 Commissioner Sir Leon Brittan had proposed that both the European Union and the United States should eliminate subsidies for the export of agricultural products to Central and Eastern Europe, Russia and the NIS. These subsidies were undermining Central and Eastern European agriculture in two ways: first, by destroying the domestic market for home-grown produce (since most CEE countries had sharply cut subsidies to their own farmers); and second, by pushing CEE produce out of its traditional export markets to the east. But the proposal was considered to be too controversial and was therefore not presented to the Washington summit for further consideration. The US Mission to the European Union favored engaging the EU in a discussion of how to develop a common position on the treatment of Central Europe for rules of origin purposes because it would promote the elimination of trade barriers between the members of the Central European Free Trade Area. Although the European Commission was originally in favor of the proposal, the European textile industry buried it.

The three working groups were tentative steps to add greater structure and substance to the US-EU relationship. The experience of these groups reconfirmed the importance of tying the many threads of the relationship into one tapestry illustrating progress from consultation to joint action. The effort to weave that tapestry became known as the New Transatlantic Agenda.

6 The genesis of the New Transatlantic Agenda

The New Transatlantic Agenda was born of common concerns in Europe and the United States, as well as concerns specific to each. After the fall of the Berlin Wall, a growing chorus of leaders and commentators in Europe expressed concern that the end of the Cold War would weaken the transatlantic link by diminishing the importance of Washington's security guarantee which had underpinned US-European relations since 1945. During his visit to the Washington in March 1995 Belgian Prime Minister Dehaene reiterated this point of view:

> The Cold War is over now. Very fortunately so, but at the same time...we have been deprived of an enemy. The glue which kept us together for so long, has lost its strength.[1]

Many other European leaders, including British Foreign Secretary Malcolm Rifkind, German Foreign Minister Genscher, French Foreign Minister Alain Juppé and European Commission President Jacques Santer, expressed similar thoughts. In the United States, House Speaker Newt Gingrich declared that only a transatlantic free trade agreement would help keep the US and Europe together:

[w]e will drift apart unless we have projects large enough to hold us together...We're not going to stay together out of nostalgia...And my suggestion is that we want to start looking at a free trade zone that includes the US and Europe...[2]

President Clinton's emphasis on domestic economic and social renewal, and US free trade initiatives with Asia (APEC) and Latin America (NAFTA and the Free Trade Agreement of the Americas), were widely misinterpreted in Europe as being further evidence of a drift of the United States from Europe. Although this perception could be partly ascribed to the recurrent bouts of angst in Europe about America's European orientation which have repeatedly characterized transatlantic relations, it also reflected the turn of the US Congress toward isolationism and unilateralism after the November 1994 elections, as well as the reality that US-EU relations could not effectively compete for the attention of top US decision-makers at a time of numerous foreign policy crises -- for example in Somalia, Haiti, Iraq/Kuwait and, above all, Bosnia.

The perception of transatlantic "drift" was reinforced during the course of 1994 by nagging disagreements: for example, over the Bosnian conflict, the pace and mechanics of NATO expansion, the bailout package for Mexico which Washington put together (after minimal consultation with its allies) in response to the peso crisis, the precipitous decline of the dollar, the US threat to retaliate under Section 301 of its 1974 Trade Act against the EU's banana regime, and the nomination of a successor to Peter Sutherland as head of the World Trade Organization.

In light of the generally perceived weakness of CFSP and the inability of the EU to respond effectively to the Bosnian crisis, moreover, the New Transatlantic Agenda had the potential to enhance the EU's weak foreign policy profile and to stress the global nature of its activities and aspirations. That this was a major European motivation for dedicating significant diplomatic resources to the initiative became particularly evident during the subsequent drafting sessions of the Senior Level Group consisting of high-ranking US and EU officials.

The American members in the group expressed the Administration's strong preference for a short, pithy document enumerating several priority areas for transatlantic cooperation; several of these participants favored repeating the approach adopted in the Summit of the Asia Pacific Economic Cooperation forum (APEC) and Summit of the Americas which defined concrete commitments accompanied by specific dates by which they had to be achieved. From the Administration's perspective, such an action-oriented document would have been the most effective way of responding to the cynicism which had built up, not only in the US but also in Europe, about the utility of semi-annual US-EU summits characterized by vague discussions without practical follow-up, as well as about the rhetoric in the 1990 Transatlantic Declaration.

However, the European participants insisted that the Agenda needed to be comprehensive and correspondingly lengthy in order to give full recognition to the EU's global reach. There was another, purely procedural, reason why in September 1995 the EU tabled a gargantuan draft Agenda of roughly 50 single-spaced pages reading more like a laundry-list than a plan establishing priorities for immediate action: in order to ensure speedy approval of the Agenda by the Community institutions, including the Council of Ministers and the Parliament, as well as the national governments, the Commission felt compelled to include every party's favorite program or priority for transatlantic cooperation. Subsequently, once the "grab bag" of initiatives had been approved by the relevant parties, the Commission repeatedly invoked the practical impossibility of submitting a revised text for approval before the Madrid Summit as a method of staving off proposed edits and modifications from the US side.

Other revealing differences in approach surfaced during early meetings between the two sides on the purpose and scope of the Agenda. One of the most significant of these was related to how the text of the Agenda should be organized: while the American participants had initially envisaged distinguishing between the ways in which the US and the EU cooperate in Europe from the ways they cooperate in the rest of the world, the European participants insisted that the areas of cooperation should be organized thematically, rather than geographically, in order to avoid echoing Kissinger's disdainful portrayal of Europe as a regional power. Memories of the ill-fated "Year of Europe" appeared not to have faded away!

The European Commission, in particular, saw in the Agenda an opportunity to shape a broad EU relationship with the US; this was one of the reasons for France's lukewarm attitude toward the three working groups during its EU presidency in the first half of 1995. Sir Leon Brittan was particularly eager to promote the initiative -- and even instructed Colin Budd, his Chef de Cabinet, to work full time on it during the fall of 1995 -- because it offered him a conspicuous international stage.[3] The Commission found an effective ally in Spain's ruling Socialist Party, which saw in the Agenda an opportunity to improve its image in the face of domestic political scandals and to contribute to a successful EU presidency by bringing President Clinton to Madrid for a major summit attracting international press attention.

The factors generating interest in the United States in the New Transatlantic Agenda were rather different. Europeanists within the Clinton Administration have not, by and large, believed that the United States is drifting away from Europe. However, many have been preoccupied by the potential threat that transatlantic trade disputes may reemerge as major irritants in the transatlantic relationship (as they were before the Uruguay Round) if they cease to be imbedded in a broader relationship. As trade gradually assumes a higher profile than security in transatlantic relations, according to this view, NATO is destined to lose some of the utility it has had as the central institution for promoting and symbolizing common interests. According to this view, there is therefore a need to update and reinforce the structures of transatlantic cooperation which were forged during the Cold War.[4]

Drawing principally on these themes, the US Mission to the European Union, and Ambassador Stuart Eizenstat in particular, actively urged the Administration in the early months of 1995 to elaborate a major transatlantic initiative. One of the main reasons why the White House was immediately receptive to the proposal and took a close interest in its evolution thereafter had to do with domestic politics: following the election of hostile Republic majorities in the House and Senate in November 1994, the White House found that its room for maneuver on its domestic agenda had become rather restricted and that foreign policy had become doubly important as an arena for the president to look "presidential." The proposal also appealed to those within the Administration who felt that Clinton, as the nation's first post-Cold War president and the leader of the Free World, needed to articulate a vision of US foreign policy and a New World Order in which the containment of Soviet power ceased to play a predominant role. An important part of this vision was a Europe united around the principles of democracy and free markets and of a larger transatlantic community embracing Central and Eastern Europe through its integration into Western institutions. Inspired by the history of the transatlantic partnership, which had been the strongest force in the world over the last half century for the strengthening of democracy, the liberalization of trade and the promotion of global development and prosperity, the Administration sought to identify those areas where the US and EU could supplement their consultations with joint actions to achieve common objectives.

Elaborating on proposals made by Sir Leon Brittan for a "building block" approach to transatlantic trade liberalization in the short-to-medium term through the reduction or elimination of regulatory obstacles,[5] as well as themes elaborated by the US Mission to the European Union, Secretary of State Warren Christopher delivered a major foreign policy address in Madrid on 2 June 1995 calling for a major transatlantic effort to define a framework for broad US-EU cooperation extending beyond trade:

[b]y the end of the year, we should have developed a broad-ranging transatlantic agenda for the new century -- an agenda for common economic and political action to expand democracy, prosperity and stability.[6]

His recommendation that a 'Senior Level Group' be appointed to carry out this task was approved at the US-EU Summit in Washington on 14 June. At the press conference following the summit, President Clinton echoed the Secretary's speech by stating that over the next six months the United States looked forward "to working together with our European partners to develop a common economic and political agenda for the 21st century."

The New Transatlantic Agenda also responded to the perception in Washington that the US-EU relationship should be adapted to reflect the EU's newly acquired powers under the Maastricht Treaty, particularly those aimed at achieving a Common Foreign and Security Policy and an Economic and Monetary Union. The need for a structured transatlantic relationship was becoming increasingly important as the Member States pooled ever more economic and political competencies in the EU. Although the United States has had regularly scheduled summits and consultations with many of its allies, including Canada, Mexico and Japan, relations with the European Union appeared to require greater coordination within the US Government and a specific diplomatic initiative: in addition to being the United States' largest trading partner and most important political ally, the EU poses unique challenges to US foreign policy because it is a *sui generis* entity without precedent in political history in which sovereignty has been pooled in some areas but not in others and in which the balance between intergovernmentalism, federalism and supranationalism is constantly evolving.

By defining a wide range of collaborative projects between the US and the EU in Europe and globally, the New Transatlantic Agenda also served to encourage the EU to assume greater international responsibility. The United States had already been pushing the EU in this direction for some time: for instance, the Bush Administration had urged the EU to assume primary responsibility for assistance to Central and Eastern Europe after the fall of the Berlin Wall and had supported its desire to lead international efforts at resolving the crisis in the former Yugoslavia. The EU's timid approach to the integration of Central Europe and its inability to cope with the conflict in Bosnia underscored the need for an initiative that would encourage the EU to apply its financial and diplomatic resources internationally in partnership with the United States.

The New Transatlantic Agenda also presented a way for Washington to forge a partnership with the EU on international trade policy toward third countries. The need for greater collaboration on setting the terms for the entry of Russia and China into the WTO or on improving market access to the rapidly growing economies in Asia for example, was self-evident. While both the European Union and the United States wish to redress their chronic and growing trade deficits with Asia, and even agree that hidden market barriers are the most important cause of these deficits, however, their tactics differ and occasionally work at cross-purposes. The EU has often been unwilling to support US trade initiatives aimed at improving access to key markets, such as Japan, China, South Korea, Taiwan and Malaysia. This unwillingness has exasperated some of the Administration's leading trade officials: according to Jeffrey Garten, for example, "The European Union has had a tendency to define its policy as the opposite of ours, even as it seeks virtually the same objectives."[7] From Washington's perspective, the EU's strategy has been to let the United States take on the unpopular task of opening closed markets through threats of retaliation; after criticizing Washington for undermining the multilateral order and seeking to curry favor with the targets of such threats, the EU nonetheless benefits from the improved market access negotiated by Washington.[8]

Although strengthened transatlantic relations clearly responded to a need, launching a major new initiative just before the opening of the Inter-Governmental Conference was clearly a risk: the EU might become entirely self-absorbed with the task of defining the proper balance between inter-governmentalism and supranationalism within the Union; even if the EU had sufficient energy to devote to the initiative, it was uncertain whether the Member States would permit the Community, and the Commission in particular, to enhance its foreign policy profile. Indeed, the near failure of Maastricht ratification and growing opposition, including within the signatories to the Treaty of Rome, to further European economic and political integration indicated that the Conference might impose limits on the expansion of the Community's competence and maintain the dominance of Member States over foreign and security policy.

Notwithstanding this danger, Europeanists within the Administration were generally of the view that the United States should not wait until the end of the IGC in 1997 before beginning to engage the EU in a more structured partnership: key US interests, including NATO and EU enlargement, the stabilization of the new democracies and market economies of the former Soviet bloc, the opening of new export markets and the stabilization of the Third World were at stake in the short term. At the same time, however, the experience with the Berlin working groups confirmed that engaging the EU on some of the areas over which the Member States retained competence under the Maastricht Treaty would be a slow and laborious process.

Although the motivations of the US and EU to engage in the New Transatlantic Agenda were partly distinct, as outlined above, they were also partly identical. The critical motivation for a strengthened transatlantic partnership arose from the common conviction that the most pressing problems facing the US and the EU in an increasingly interdependent world are of a transnational character and cannot be addressed satisfactorily by either acting alone. These problems include the promotion of economic growth and the creation of jobs through trade liberalization; combating international crime, terrorism, and the proliferation of weapons of mass destruction; preventing environmental degradation; and responding effectively to humanitarian crises (such as the ethnic warfare in Rwanda or the outbreak of the Ebola virus in Zaire). Several influential associations of European and American business and government leaders, particularly the Transatlantic Policy Network, had long been advocating a coordinated transatlantic approach to many of these problems.

Shrinking foreign affairs budgets on both sides of the Atlantic -- resulting from efforts to reduce public debt and government deficits -- have convinced many policy makers that independent action to address transnational crises is a wasteful luxury of the past. After the election in the November 1994 Congressional elections of hostile Republic majorities which endorsed isolationist or unilateralist foreign policies, the Clinton Administration came under particularly severe pressure to further reduce the budget for the State Department and Agency for International Development (AID). The New Transatlantic Agenda offered the prospect of helping the United States to maintain its superpower status "on the cheap" in the 1990s.

The Agenda was also perceived by the executive branches officials on both sides of the Atlantic as a useful mechanism to launch quickly a major transatlantic initiative which would not require lengthy parliamentary ratification. A two European Commission officials who were key players in the elaboration of the Agenda have accurately observed:

> In a situation where leaders on both sides of the Atlantic intended to send a political signal rapidly, an instrument which did not have to be submitted to the long and sometimes complicated approval procedures of the US Congress, the European Parliament and all the Parliaments of the Member States of the European Union was very attractive.[9]

Had the Agenda been submitted for parliamentary ratification, it is by no means certain that it would have been approved. Unlike the French government, the French Parliament, for example, might not have been willing to compromise on its fierce opposition to the idea of further tariff reduction; similarly, those members of the House of Representatives and Senate, elected in November 1994, who believed that the United States should retreat into isolation or only act unilaterally abroad would certainly have objected to the spirit and initiatives set forth in the Agenda.

By establishing a framework and concrete objectives for transatlantic dialogue, the New Transatlantic Agenda responded to the concerns of those on both sides of the Atlantic that the sense of common commitment and mutual attachment of Europe and the United States might fade with the rise of a new generation of leaders born after the War. As one of the leading American commentators on Europe observed:

> Many of the 'old Atlanticists' are growing old, and not enough is being done to reproduce the ease of communication they gradually learned. It wasn't easy to get this far. It would be a grievous loss to let the capacity fade away. *The one permanent certainty about the future is that it will bring mutual problems to solve.*[10]

Nostalgia about the commonality of interests, values and traditions in the United States and Europe was clearly no substitute for closer collaboration. The 1990 Transatlantic Declaration and the Berlin working groups were tentative steps in this direction, but had not gone far enough. The New Transatlantic Agenda negotiated by the Senior Level Group therefore filled an important need.

Notes

1   Speech to the European Institute, March 1995.

2   Quoted in Glennon Harrison, "A New Transatlantic Initiative? US-EU Economic Relations in the Mid-1990s," CRS Report for Congress, 15 September 1995. Speech by Speaker Gingrich, "An American Vision for the 21st Century," delivered at the Mayflower Hotel, 1 March 1995.

3   Critics claimed that Brittan's secret agenda was to reassert his influence over the EU's relations with Central and Eastern Europe which he had lost to Commissioner van den Broek during the Commission's reshuffling of portfolios in January 1995.

4   The European Commission also expressed this view: "The US-EU relationship...cannot be relied upon to function in the future on the basis of structures and priorities relevant to the Cold War era." European Commission, "Europe and the United States: The Way Forward," July 1995.

5   "The EU-US Relationship: Will it Last?," Speech to the American Club in Brussels, 27 April 1995.

6   US Department of State, 'Charting a Transatlantic Agenda for the 21st Century,' Madrid, Spain, 2 June 1995.

7   Under-Secretary of Commerce Jeffrey Garten, Speech to the European Institute, 9 May 1995.

8   This is still a strongly felt view among leading US observers of the EU. At a farewell address at the American Chamber or Commerce in Brussels before leaving his post as US Ambassador to the EU, for example, Stuart Eizenstat stated: "We find ourselves out front, along, negotiating everything from intellectual property agreements with China to a set of sectoral agreements with Japan, extending them on a most-favored nation basis to the rest of the world, and finding European companies walking into the doors we open." See "Brussels Trade Pacts 'Corrosive,'" *The Financial Times*, 9 February 1996.

9   Horst Krenzler and Astrid Schomaker, "A New Transatlantic Agenda," *European Foreign Affairs Review*, Vol. 1, No. 1, July 1996, p. 18.

10   Flora Lewis, "Atlantic Connections Begin to Fray," *International Herald Tribune*, 23 June 1995. Emphasis added.

7 The New Transatlantic Agenda

The New Transatlantic Agenda signed at the US-EU Summit in Madrid on 3 December reaffirms the centrality of the US-EU partnership and underlines the desire of both sides to move from consultation to joint action in four priority areas between the Madrid Summit and the following summit in Washington under Italy's EU presidency. A second, much lengthier document, entitled the "Joint US-EU Action Plan," which was not signed at the summit but which was negotiated and agreed to by the two sides, sets forth roughly 150 longer term objectives from which a number will be selected for the regular updating of the Agenda between subsequent US-EU summits.

The Agenda describes four priority areas for US-EU collaboration:
1 Promoting Peace and Stability, Democracy and Development Around the World;
2 Responding to Global Challenges;
3 Contributing to the Expansion of World Trade and Closer Economic Relations; and
4 Building Bridges Across the Atlantic.

Promoting peace and stability, democracy and development around the world

The most immediate priority for cooperation set forth under this heading is to implement the Dayton Accords (particularly those provisions relating to arms control, disarmament, confidence-building, the protection of human rights and the holding of free and fair elections), as well as to assist in the reconstruction of the Former Yugoslavia.

The text in both the Agenda and Action Plan regarding financial assistance to the reconstruction of the Former Yugoslavia was the subject of considerable negotiation in the Senior Level Group:

> ...we will contribute to the task of reconstruction... in the context of the widest possible burden-sharing with other donors and taking advantage of the experience of international institutions, of the European Commission and of all relevant bilateral donors in the coordination mechanism.

This language masked profound differences between the US and EU regarding the share of the burden which they should each bear. From Washington's perspective, naturally, the European Union should contribute more than the United States to the costs of reconstruction. As the Former Yugoslavia is on Europe's doorstep but distant from the United States, Europe has a greater stake in the successful implementation of the peace; indeed, following the outbreak of the conflict in 1991, numerous European leaders invoked Europe's special interests in the region to argue that Europe rather than the United States should assume primary responsibility.

The Clinton Administration has pledged to pay less than a one third share ($500-600 million over three years) of the estimated cost of reconstruction ($3 billion) and has sought to convince the EU to pay more than a one third share. After having devoted enormous diplomatic resources, and military muscle, to achieve the Dayton Accords and having pledged 20,000 troops to help implement its terms, there is little desire in Washington to do more to 'pull Europe's chestnuts out of the fire.' Obtaining Congressional approval for the stationing of troops in the Former Yugoslavia was difficult enough for the Administration; requesting the appropriation of $1 billion or more for reconstruction in the middle of acrimonious disagreements on how to balance the federal government's budget would have been politically impossible.

A second priority for US-EU cooperation set forth in the Agenda and Action Plan is to support the Middle East peace process, as well as Palestinian self-government and economic development, by implementing the conclusions of the Casablanca and Amman Economic Summits and the pledging Conference for Economic Assistance to the Palestinians, coordinating US and EU assistance programs, improving the access granted by both to products from the West Bank and Gaza Strip, encouraging free trade agreements between Israel, Jordan, Egypt and the Palestinian Authority, and working together to end the Arab boycott of Israel.

A third priority is to reinforce US-EU coordination of technical and financial assistance to consolidate democratic and market reforms in Central and Eastern Europe, Russia and the New Independent States. Building on ideas that had been discussed in the Berlin working groups, the Action Plan calls for 'regular and intensified contacts' between US embassies and Commission Delegations to ensure proper coordination of assistance in the region and to support environmental protection in CEE through the Budapest Regional Environmental Center and in the NIS through the establishment of a similar institution.

Whereas the US and EU pledge in the Agenda and Action Plan only to support the integration of Russia, Ukraine and other NIS states into the *global economy*, they pledge to support the integration of Central and Eastern Europe into international *political and economic institutions*. From Washington's perspective, the language with regard to the latter does not go far enough because it fails to recognize the EU's special role in stabilizing the region economically and politically: the United States has played the leadership role in NATO and NATO enlargement; now it is up to the EU to exercise comparable leadership through early eastward enlargement.

Although a reference in the Agenda and Action Plan to the mechanics and timing of EU enlargement would have been inappropriate because enlargement is a matter internal to the EU and therefore not a proper subject for joint US-EU action, the documents could have reflected Washington's concerns by explicitly laying forth a common vision of a transatlantic community encompassing Central and Eastern Europe. That would have been an important message strengthening the resolve of the people in the region to persevere with painful reforms. Yet the EU succeeded in keeping the focus of the documents on the US-EU relationship rather than on the relationship between the US and an evolving Europe.

A fourth priority is to improve coordination of humanitarian assistance programs and preventive and crisis diplomacy. The US and EU pledge in the Agenda and Action Plan to establish a High-Level Consultative Group on Development Cooperation and Humanitarian Assistance which will meet alternately in Brussels and Washington to exchange information and coordinate policies, from the stage of planning to that of execution, in order to support democracy and civil society; food security; sustainable development and economic reform; and the work of international humanitarian relief agencies, such as the UN High Commission for Refugees, the World Food Program and the UN's Department of Humanitarian Affairs. The Action Plan also calls for regular and intensified contacts between US missions and European Commission delegations to improve cooperation on humanitarian assistance programs. The brain-child of Brian Atwood, Director of USAID, and Emma Bonino, Commissioner in charge of the EU's humanitarian aid program, the central objective of the initiative is to avoid wasteful overlap and maximize existing resources in an era of budget austerity.

Responding to global challenges

The immediate priority under this heading is to coordinate policies to combat international crime, trafficking in drugs and nuclear materials and terrorism which threaten to undermine the nascent democracies in the NIS and CEE and endanger the security of individuals throughout the world.

In the Agenda and Action Plan the US and EU pledge to:

1   promote the rule of law by supporting existing regional law enforcement and judicial training centers, such as the International Law Academy in Budapest (training of mid-level police officers in CEE and the NIS) and the Italian Judicial Training Centre (training of judges in CEE and the NIS), as well as by establishing new such centers;
2   establish an information exchange mechanism between the US and EU and its member states in the law enforcement and criminal justice fields;
3   implement the provisions of the European Police (EUROPOL) Convention to facilitate relations between the US Government and EUROPOL, once it is in operation;[1]
4   strengthen the Dublin Group (coordinating international anti-drug trafficking measures) by reinforcing its members' counter-narcotic efforts; and
5   strengthen international mechanisms for obtaining evidence, facilitating judicial seizure and forfeiture of assets used in or resulting from the commission of crimes, and simplifying extradition and deportation procedures.

The continuing inability of EU Member States to cooperate amongst themselves in the fight against international drug trafficking and crime is likely to impede progress on this part of the Agenda in the near future. Most seriously, the United Kingdom has threatened to block agreement on a convention governing EUROPOL because it opposes European Court of Justice oversight over the latter's operations. Failure to advance "Third Pillar" cooperation on home and justice affairs in 1995 and 1996 has contributed to the troubles of the Schengen Convention, an intergovernmental agreement outside of EU jurisdiction to abolish identity controls at internal borders between seven EU countries.[2] Soon after his election in May 1995, President Chirac withdrew France from the Schengen Group in response to terrorist attacks in France and in protest at the Netherlands' permissive policy toward "soft" drugs. Although France subsequently dropped border controls with Spain and Germany, it was continuing to enforce such controls with the Benelux through mid-1996. In February 1996, Spain threatened to withdraw from the Schengen Group following the decision by Belgium's highest court to refuse Spain's request to extradite two suspected ETA (Basque) terrorists.   Despite these failures, however, officials in the Clinton Administration remain hopeful that the New Transatlantic Agenda may contribute to improved intra-European coordination on "Third Pillar" issues by placing emphasis on transatlantic cooperation on international crime and drug trafficking.

Transatlantic frictions over the means of combatting international crime have also highlighted how difficult it will be to make progress on the part of the Agenda dedicated to "Third Pillar" collaboration.   The effectiveness of international cooperation on crime ultimately depends on the exchange of sensitive information; such an exchange, in turn, can only occur if the transmitter of the information trusts the receiving party's policies and administrative procedures on crime.   In some instances, this basis of trust is still lacking, even between those transatlantic partners where it is most urgently needed.   Of all the channels of communication which the Washington maintains with its European allies on international crime, the one it has with Italy is probably the most important given the strong links between organized crime in the United States and Italy.   US suspicions regarding the laxity of Italy's criminal justice system were recently exacerbated when a Palestinian terrorist found guilty of murdering an American on board the Italian cruise liner Achille Lauro escaped from an Italian jail while on weekend leave.   (Although the terrorist was later caught by Spanish authorities, the Italian authorities' defensive reaction to the affair dumbfounded US authorities, who simply could not comprehend how one of the world's most wanted terrorists could be granted leave without supervision).   Matters have been made even worse by a recent ruling by Italy's Constitutional Court preventing the extradition of an Italian criminal to face murder charges in the United States, despite a 1983 extradition treaty between Italy and the United States.   Refusing to acknowledge assurances by US authorities that the extradition treaty is supreme over the laws of US states, including those in Florida providing for the death penalty, the Constitutional Court found that the extradition treaty was not applicable because it would violate the criminal's right to life protected by the Italian Constitution.   As the central purpose of the extradition treaty is to facilitate the extradition of dangerous criminals so that they can stand trial in the country where the criminal act was performed, this judgment has cast doubt on the very future of the treaty and has, therefore, seriously set back Italo-American cooperation on international crime.[3]

The Agenda and Action Plan also call for enhanced bilateral consultations on the environment and closer coordination in international negotiations on the environment.   As this area is less politically charged than international crime and drug trafficking, the prospect for transatlantic cooperation in the short to medium term is rather good.   In the Agenda and Action Plan, the US and EU pledge to work together to reduce risks from hazardous substances, such as lead, and to limit and reduce emissions of greenhouse gases, including CO_2.

They further pledge to intensify their dialogue on a broad range of environmental concerns, including water purity, biotechnology, trade in hazardous chemicals, and regulatory cooperation. In seeking to address the serious environmental problems in CEE and the NIS, the US and EU will support the Regional Environmental Center in Budapest and the establishment of similar centers in Moldova, Ukraine and Russia.

As part of their joint efforts to promote political stability and sustainable economic development, the US and EU will cooperate, both bilaterally and within the framework of the World Health Organization, on health-related matters; develop a global early warning system to respond to the outbreak of communicable diseases, such as AIDS and the Ebola Virus; and encourage participation in research programs by scientists from developing countries.

Contributing to the expansion of world trade and closer economic relations

Under this heading the US and EU pledge to establish a "Transatlantic Marketplace" by reducing the barriers to the free circulation of goods, services and capital across the Atlantic. The strategy set forth in the Agenda and Action Plan to establish this marketplace consists of pledges to implement fully the Uruguay Round commitments, to accelerate Uruguay Round reductions in tariffs in certain sectors, reinforce international investment liberalization and protection, reduce technical and non-tariff barriers by improving regulatory cooperation, and carry out a joint US-EU study on how further to reduce or eliminate tariff and non-tariff barriers.

Transatlantic Free Trade Area or Transatlantic Marketplace?

The Agenda and Action Plan envisage the creation of a Transatlantic Marketplace rather than a Transatlantic Free Trade Area (TAFTA). In distinction to the latter, which focusses on the elimination of tariffs, the former is a broader concept encompassing the reduction of tariff and non-tariff barriers to the free flow of goods and services. The principle reason for this focus is that the business community on both sides of the Atlantic has made clear that non-tariff barriers, such as differences in standards and barriers to investment, are more serious obstacles to transatlantic trade than tariff barriers which have been reduced to negligible levels in most sectors following the implementation of Uruguay Round commitments. Moreover, the elimination of tariffs would be politically sensitive in several sectors in both Europe and the United States.

From Washington's perspective, the strong *foreign policy* motivations for creating a TAFTA are outweighed by *international economic and domestic political considerations.*[4] The most important foreign policy motivation is to

76

respond to the growing perception that transatlantic security ties are weakening following the end of the Cold War and that new institutions and arrangements are required to maintain Western unity. The recent conclusion of regional free trade accords, including the North American Free Trade Agreement (NAFTA) and Mercosur in the Americas, the agreement to liberalize trade and investment in the Pacific Rim by the members of the Asia Pacific Economic Cooperation forum, the web of Association Agreements (providing for free trade in all goods by 1997) between the EU and Central and Eastern Europe, and the trade agreements between the EU and selected countries in Northern Africa and the Middle East, have highlighted the irony that the US and the EU -- representing the world's greatest combined two-way flow of goods (roughly $250 billion annually) and investment (roughly $500 billion in total), as well as sharing similar levels of socioeconomic development and perspectives on trade -- are not yet partners in a free trade agreement.[5]

Nevertheless, the idea of negotiating a TAFTA in the near future has not generated much enthusiasm in the Clinton Administration because of international economic and domestic political considerations.[6] Among the most important of these are that non-tariff barriers are a greater impediment to transatlantic trade than tariff barriers; that a TAFTA might not be compatible with the WTO and might weaken the multilateral trading order; that new negotiations for across-the-board tariff reductions, unlike sector-by-sector negotiations on reducing tariff and non-tariff barriers conducted under residual presidential negotiating authority left over from the Uruguay Round, would require the President to obtain special authority from the US Congress; and that negotiating a TAFTA would strain transatlantic relations by reopening divisive issues left over from the Uruguay Round, such as agricultural protection, quotas on US audiovisual exports and aircraft subsidies, on which further progress is unlikely over the short term.

Tariff barriers, which would be the central (though not exclusive) focus of a TAFTA, are no longer a serious impediment to transatlantic trade. Although high tariffs persist in certain sensitive sectors such as agriculture, textiles and apparel, and semiconductors,[7] US exports to the EU will face average tariffs of 6.36 per cent and US imports from the EU will face average tariffs of only 3.19 per cent after the full implementation of Uruguay Round tariff cuts. The generally held view within the Administration, shared by the EU and most business leaders on both sides of the Atlantic, is that non-tariff barriers pose the most serious obstacles to freer transatlantic trade.

A TAFTA, moreover, might not be consistent with the WTO. Under GATT Article XXIV, free trade agreements must cover "substantially all trade" between the partner countries. A TAFTA which excluded agriculture might not satisfy that condition: although trade in agricultural products only accounts for 5.5 per cent of US-EU trade, it would account for a much higher percentage in the absence of subsidies and quotas on both sides of the Atlantic. Even if a TAFTA conformed to WTO rules, moreover, it might undermine the multilateral trading system: first, the trade diversion effects flowing from a free trade accord between the world's two largest trading blocs would be far more serious than similar effects from other free trade areas; second, a TAFTA which did not extend trade benefits to the rest of the world on a Most Favored Nation (MFN) basis[8] would discriminate against the world's poorer countries and thereby undermine efforts to encourage their economic development by ensuring free and non-discriminatory access to the markets of industrialized countries.[9]

Negotiating a TAFTA would also be problematic because of domestic political complications. The limited resources at USTR have already been stretched by overseeing the implementation of Uruguay Round obligations, NAFTA, and APEC; negotiating greater access to the Japanese auto and auto parts sectors; responding to the piracy of intellectual property in China and defining conditions for China's entry into the WTO; negotiating a compensation package with the EU as a result of the latter's enlargement and the resulting tariff increases in Austria, Finland and Sweden; and coping with numerous irritants in US-EU trading relations concerning bananas, beef hormones and the audiovisual sector. Even more important, protectionist sentiment and concern about the budgetary impact of foregone tariff revenues would generate considerable opposition in the US Congress to a request by the Executive Branch for 'fast-track' negotiating authority.

Finally, the Clinton Administration's lack of enthusiasm for a TAFTA reflects the fact that whereas it would only negotiate (and Congress would only ratify) an agreement which included agriculture, the EU would insist on its exclusion. In addition to being unacceptable for domestic political reasons, an agreement excluding agriculture would be less economically attractive than one which included it: the elimination of tariffs on all transatlantic trade, including agricultural products, would increase US exports to the EU by an estimated 10.8 per cent and EU exports to the US by 6.3 per cent; but the elimination of tariffs on non-agricultural goods would increase exports by only 4.1 per cent and 4.4 per cent, respectively.[10] Even if agricultural products were included within the scope of the negotiations, it is unlikely that significant progress could be reached. Such progress was possible in the context of the multilateral Uruguay Round negotiations where US-EU disputes were imbedded in a much larger context offering considerable scope for trade-offs; bilateral negotiations would highlight persistent areas of discord without providing such a context.

The trade chapter in the Action Plan

In the Action Plan the US and EU pledge, for example, to:

1   encourage cooperation on standards, both between their regulatory agencies and in international standards setting bodies, with special attention to motor vehicle safety and environmental standards;
2   conclude agreements on mutual recognition of conformity assessment (MRAs) on, *inter alia*, medical devices, telecommunications terminal equipment, and information technology products;
3   extend the coverage of US-EU bilateral commitments on public procurement and promote multilateral negotiations within the WTO covering substantially all government procurement;
4   collaborate at the Organization for Economic Cooperation and Development (OECD) to conclude a multilateral agreement on investment (MAI) promoting investment liberalization and protection; and
5   combat corruption and bribery by implementing the 1994 OECD Recommendation on Bribery in International Transactions.

Mutual recognition agreements, one of the focal points of the Action Plan, will bring about a "one stop shop" in which certain products will be tested once and thereafter accepted for sale on both sides of the Atlantic: US and European manufacturers will be able to sell these products in one another's markets after a single laboratory test, rather than having to undergo expensive and duplicative testing procedures. By reducing the time necessary for product testing by many months, this "one stop shop" will yield considerable cost savings: firms in the computer, telecommunications and business equipment industry, for example, estimate that a mutual recognition agreement in their sector could save them more than $1 billion each year.[11] By enabling companies to reduce the time from laboratory to market and to exploit economies of scale by expanding available markets, MRAs considerably reduce costs for product development and manufacture and result in a lower rate of "infant mortality" for product innovations. Unrestricted access to new products and processes is particularly important to small and medium-sized enterprises (SMEs), the traditional engines of economic growth and employment.

Discriminatory public procurement practices in Europe, the United States and around the world, particularly in the rapidly growing economies of East Asia, are non-tariff barriers of considerable concern to businesses on both sides of the Atlantic. The office of the USTR was eager to make this a priority of the Action Plan: although some federal and state laws in the United States contain "Buy American" provisions, similar discrimination on an EU or national basis allegedly covers a wider scope of economic activity. The European utilities market alone is estimated to be worth approximately $40-50 billion over the next ten years. A series of EC directives have in theory opened up procurement contracts in much of this sector to freer competition;[12] but US firms have been unable to benefit because these directives have not been fully implemented into national law and none has been fully implemented by all Member States. Moreover, US firms have been largely excluded from those sectors -- water, energy, transportation, postal and telecommunications -- which have not yet been opened up to non-discriminatory public procurement. The Action Plan commits both the US and EU to increase substantially their bilateral commitments on public procurement and to cooperate at the December 1996, WTO Ministerial meeting in Singapore to launch negotiations aimed at covering substantially all government procurement and involving a wider circle of WTO members.

Other non-tariff barriers of concern to US business, and to their European counterparts, include divergent customs procedures and trade and competition policies. The Agenda and Action Plan respond to this concern by setting forth the pledge of the US and EU to conclude a Customs Cooperation and Mutual Assistance Agreement by the end of 1996 simplifying customs procedures and promoting information exchange, as well as to pursue a second-generation US-EU agreement on competition policy.[13]

Although the Action Plan does not contain any specific commitments to eliminate tariffs in the information technology sector, the US and EU have made it a major priority to conclude at the December 1996 WTO Ministerial or shortly thereafter an Information Technology Agreement (ITA) calling for the elimination of tariffs on information technology products by the year 2000.[14] The fact that this objective is a priority reflects the considerable importance of the high-technology sector for the United States and Europe.

The computer and semiconductor industry together provide high-wage jobs for over 1.25 million Americans; despite EU tariffs of around 14 per cent, the highest in the industrialized world, in 1994 the US exported to the EU $18.5 billion worth of semiconductors, computers, software and telecommunications equipment, accounting for more than 17 per cent of total US exports to the EU. Although the EU committed itself to reduce these tariffs on information technology products to 3.5% in the Uruguay Round Final Act, several Member States have vitiated this commitment by reclassifying certain products, including personal computers and local network hardware, in order to place them into a higher duty category.[15]

Most consumer electronics manufacturers in the EU share the US desire to eliminate tariffs on semiconductors in order to reduce the cost of important components.[16] Major users of telecommunications services, who pay far higher bills than their competitors across the Atlantic, also have an interest in a more competitive market for information technology products and telecommunications equipment. Lower tariffs would promote the European Commission's agenda for trade liberalization and economic growth stimulation in high value-added sectors. The prospects of achieving an ITA by the end of 1996 have been complicated, however, by French opposition to tariff reductions and by the EU's linkage of the ITA to the future of the 1991 US-Japan Semiconductor Arrangement which has reserved 20 per cent of Japan's chip market to foreign suppliers.[17] In mid-1996 Sir Leon Brittan, the EU's Commissioner in charge of external trade relations, warned that the EU would not sign the ITA if the bilateral agreement, due to expire at the end of July 1996, was renewed without being multilateralized; the EU, moreover, has consistently opposed all preconditions, including the elimination of tariffs, to the multilateralization of the agreement. The follow-on agreement negotiated between the US and Japan in Vancouver at the end of July 1996 achieved only part of this objective: while the EU will be allowed to participate in a global government forum to discuss worldwide semiconductor industry issues including tariffs, taxation and environmental rules, the forum will play only the limited role of meeting occasionally to discuss information on sales and market shares gathered by a newly-formed private-sector council of semiconductor industry associations from the US and Japan. The forum will not be able to hold the Japanese to any pledges to continue buying foreign chips or to discourage the sale of chips on the US market at below the cost of production in Japan. The private-sector council will play a far more significant role: in addition to monitoring the foreign share of Japan's semiconductor market, it will promote industrial cooperation, such as joint ventures. In order to participate in the council, the EU must agree to eliminate its semiconductor tariffs.

Related to the ITA are efforts, mentioned in the Action Plan, to create a Transatlantic Information Society through greater interoperability and interconnection of information technology systems, and harmonized policies regarding competition, privacy and data protection, access to information and intellectual property protection.[18]

In addition to seeking the reduction of tariff and non-tariff barriers across the Atlantic, the Clinton Administration saw the New Transatlantic Agenda as an opportunity to help ensure that EU firms observe fair business practices, particularly in the growing and lucrative markets of Asia and Latin America. Whereas payoffs to foreign officials are tax deductible in many EU Member States, US firms which provide them may be criminally sanctioned under the 1977 Foreign Corrupt Practices Act. In the Agenda the US and EU pledge to implement the 1994 OECD Recommendation banning such tax deductibility. But the Office of the USTR, which estimates that foreign bribes undercut American firms for tens of billions of dollars of contracts each year, has reserved the right to apply Section 301 sanctions against those countries which fail to prevent their companies from giving bribes to win contracts overseas.

On one economic item in the New Transatlantic Agenda, there was considerable disagreement. France insisted that the EU negotiate with Washington language calling for measures to foster greater monetary stability. This has been a familiar French refrain for several decades: efforts to reduce barriers to trade are of limited value, so the argument goes, if exchange rates fluctuate significantly. Although this is of course true, the Clinton Administration rejects the accusation that it has used the dollar as a trade weapon; it argues that the decline in the dollar reflects certain underlying economic fundamentals. It is these fundamentals -- above all the budget deficit -- which are the focus of the Administration's economic policy. At the time the Agenda was being drafted, the US Treasury therefore insisted that the Agenda merely refer to transatlantic discussions concerning economic fundamentals which have an impact on macroeconomic policy. It rejected any language suggesting coordinated intervention in the currency markets and continues to oppose the idea (still popular in France) of reverting to fixed exchange rates. In any event, the appreciation of the dollar in the first half of 1996 will presumably temper French concerns to discuss monetary issues within the context of the Agenda.

Building bridges across the Atlantic

The fourth and final chapter of the Agenda and Action Plan includes pledges to deepen transatlantic cultural, scientific, and educational ties. Although this heading is short on specifics, the people-to-people links which it calls for -- such as greater exchange programs and cooperative science and technology projects -- may well prove to be as significant as other initiatives in the long term, as it will broaden the basis of the transatlantic partnership and, as a result, help ensure that Europe and the United States remain closely linked in the post-Cold War era.

The recently concluded US-EU Agreement on Cooperation in Higher Education and Vocational Training, which will create consortia of universities and other institutions on both sides of the Atlantic, is a concrete step toward creating transatlantic "educational networks." In the Action Plan, moreover, the US and EU pledge to encourage private support for educational exchanges, scholarship and intern programs, to promote the study of each other's systems of government, cultures and languages, to facilitate the mutual recognition of university studies and degrees, and to examine ways of employing new technologies to link education and training establishments on both sides of the Atlantic. Both sides have also endorsed the idea of strengthening relations between elected representatives in the US and Europe, although it will be the representatives themselves who will determine the form which this initiative will take.

Under the fourth chapter of the Agenda the US and EU also pledge to promote the Transatlantic Business Dialogue (TABD) launched at the initiative of Secretary of Commerce Ron Brown and EU Commissioners Sir Leon Brittan and Martin Bangemann at Seville on 11 November 1995, with the participation of leading representatives of the business world in Europe and the US. The initiative reflects the reality that business is best placed to assess which barriers to transatlantic trade cause the greatest difficulties in practice and therefore to propose priorities for future government-to-government trade negotiations. One of the main attractions of the TABD is that it "depoliticizes" US-EU trade relations by providing an unofficial forum for the formulation of maximum private-sector consensus on practical solutions to pressing trade problems. These relations have often been driven in the past by the lobbying efforts of domestic constituencies -- usually an industry or even one company -- aggrieved by certain trade policies or practices on the other side of the Atlantic. Responding to this pressure, US and EU trade officials have often engaged in mutual recriminations which attract considerable publicity and sour both economic and political transatlantic relations. The Seville conference produced more than 70 specific recommendations for government action in the areas of standards, certification and regulatory policy, trade liberalization, investment and third country cooperation. Many of these recommendations were incorporated in the Agenda and Action Plan.

Notes

1   The European Drugs Unit (EDU), the forerunner of EUROPOL, is based in The Hague and is staffed mainly by liaison officers working for their home governments. The activity of the agency has been limited to exchanging information and enhancing coordination in the fight against trafficking in drugs and nuclear materials and car theft. Ratification of the EUROPOL Convention is currently being blocked by the United Kingdom.

2   The countries are Belgium, France, Germany, Luxembourg, The Netherlands, Portugal and Spain. Austria, Greece and Italy are expected to become full members. In early 1996, however, the new Greek government threatened not to sign the Schengen Convention on the ground that its computerized information system would violate

Greek personal privacy laws. Austria and Italy, original signatories of the convention, had failed to make the Convention operational by mid-1996. The United Kingdom and Ireland have decided not to join. Denmark, Finland and Sweden are expected to become full members by the end of 1996. Iceland and Norway will become associate members of Schengen, participating fully in its implementation but not having voting rights.

3   See Robert Graham, "Allies At Odds Over Extradition," *The Financial Times*, 8 July 1996.

4   The European Commission also appears to give particular importance to the political aspects of concluding FTAs. In a Communication to the Council it stated that "Conveying a clear political message to a country regarding its importance for the Union also remains a motivation for proposing an FTA...[p]olitical considerations are as important as the potential economic benefits and in some cases may be the primary motivation. FTAs are coming to be seen as an indicator of the strength of our relationship with a country or region." See "Free Trade Areas: An Appraisal," Communication from the Commission to the Council, IP/95/215, 8 March 1995.

5   Statistics from US Department of Commerce, Survey of Current Business, June 1995.

6   Press commentary on the New Transatlantic Agenda generally appreciated this fact. The outstanding exception was France, where the French press suspected that the United States was in favor of a TAFTA as a way to dismantle the Common Agricultural Policy and EU restrictions on US audiovisual exports.

7   Tariffs on textiles and apparel are above 20 per cent in the US and 11-12 per cent on average in the EU; tariffs on semiconductors are non-existent in the US and 10-14 per cent in the EU; and the tariff equivalents of agricultural products after the full implementation of Uruguay Round reforms will be 30 per cent in the US and 75 per cent in the EU. Jeffrey Schott, "Reflections on TAFTA," Unpublished Paper delivered before the Council on Foreign Relations, 19 June 1995.

8   If the objective were to extend trade benefits under a TAFTA to third countries on an MFN basis, it would appear more logical to pursue multilateral trade negotiations for global trade liberalization.

9   In a major foreign policy speech in Madrid on 2 June 1995, Secretary of State Christopher stated that the United States would conduct a study of the implications of a transatlantic free trade agreement, but cautioned that the Administration would only support such an agreement if it satisfied three stringent conditions: it would have to "advance our overring objective of global trade liberalization, be consistent with an effective WTO, and not disadvantage less developed countries." US Department of State, 'Charting a Transatlantic Agenda for the 21st Century,' Madrid, Spain, 2 June 1995.

10   Jeffrey Schott, 'Reflections on TAFTA,' Unpublished Paper delivered before the Council on Foreign Relations, 19 June 1995. The percentage figures roughly correspond to an increase of US exports of $8 billion per year.

11   "The Future of Transatlantic Trade Relations," US Chamber of Commerce Background Papers and Recommendations for the Transatlantic Business Dialogue Conference in Seville.

12   The competition is freer, rather than free, as a result of these directives. The Utilities Directive allows continued discrimination against non-EU bids by containing a mandatory buy-Europe provision requiring bids to meet a 50 per cent local content provision and allowing national public authorities to accept EU bids that are 3 per cent higher in price than those put forward by non-EU companies.

13   The 1991 Antitrust Cooperation Agreement between the EU, on the one hand, and the Department of Justice and Federal Trade Commission, on the other, provides for the exchange of information and cooperation between these authorities. The cooperation foreseen in the Agreement includes notification of enforcement activities that may affect important interests of the other party; coordination of enforcement activities where the parties agree that it is in their mutual interest to do so; and consideration of comity in enforcement decisions.

14   The products covered by such an agreements might cover some or even all of the following: computer hardware (including computer peripherals and multimedia / multifunctional products), semi-conductor manufacturing equipment, computer and telecommunications software, telecommunications equipment, parts and accessories.

15   By classifying personal computers that can be used as televisions (PCTVs) as consumer electronics, the United Kingdom subjected them to a 14 per cent import tariff. Ireland subjected networking equipment to a 7.5 per cent import tariff by reclassifying it as telecommunications equipment.

16   Section II.8 of the Transatlantic Business Dialogue Conclusions declares that "It is the view of the overwhelming majority that the ITA package should include a commitment to eliminate tariffs by 1 January 2000 or sooner."

17   Although the agreement reserves 20 per cent of the Japanese market for *foreign* firms, in reality it has served to preserve that slice for US firms. The foreign share of the $44 billion Japanese semi-conductor market stood at roughly 30 per cent in mid-1996. Of this slice, US firms had 19 per cent, South Korean firms 9 per cent and European firms 1.5 per cent. When the original agreement was signed in 1986, foreign firms only had a market share of 8 per cent.

18   These issues have already been the subject of an "Information Society Dialogue" between senior US and EU telecoms officials under the auspices of the 'sub-cabinet' consultative process.

8 An interim report card

President Clinton concluded the December 1995 US-EU summit in Madrid by stating that the Transatlantic Agenda would ultimately be judged according to its practical results rather than its aspirations and that the following summit in Washington at the end of the Italian presidency should draw up an interim "report card" on the Agenda's progress. The US-EU summit in Washington on 12 June 1996, therefore, offers a logical perspective from which to assess the first six months of progress and to reflect on the significance of the Agenda over the longer term.

At the June summit President Clinton, Italian Prime Minister Romano Prodi and President Santer were naturally upbeat about the progress which had been achieved thus far under the Agenda. President Clinton declared that "We can take pride that this transatlantic agenda has made a strong start"; Prime Minister Prodi noted that "This has been a very effective semester"; and President Santer stated that the summit marked a "first milestone" in "a new, deeper and more robust relationship between Europe and America than in the past." To what extent did the record support these claims? Although the summit was indeed able to register some important results over the previous six months under each of the four chapters of the Agenda, participants on both sides agreed that the achievements had fallen far short of the expectations harbored at the Madrid summit.[1]

The achievements

Under the first chapter of the Agenda on "Promoting Peace, Stability, Democracy and Development Around the World," the US and the EU have begun to create a network of environmental centers in Russia, the Ukraine and the NIS and to coordinate their development and humanitarian assistance programs, including by means of aligning their budgets to avoid having different financial years create gaps in aid coverage for those countries receiving assistance from both the United States and Europe and by means of carrying out joint missions (such as to Rwanda and Burundi) to assess specific regions' humanitarian needs. The US and the EU agreed, moreover, to hold trilateral consultations with the UN High Commissioner for Refugees Sadako Ogata. In the six months since the December summit in Madrid, the US and the EU cooperated in implementing the Dayton accords by ensuring a successful donors' conference in April 1996 on reconstruction of the former Yugoslavia, worked together with the the Organization for Security and Cooperation in Europe to support human rights monitors and prepare for Bosnian elections, and have co-funded specific projects, such as a UN demining center in Sarajevo.

Under the second chapter of the Agenda on "Responding to Global Challenges," the US and the EU have made some progress on the issues of international crime, health and the environment. On the first of these, they have concluded an agreement to control trade in dangerous chemicals and illegal drugs. With regard to international health, they have established a joint Task Force on Communicable Diseases to deploy an early warning network to respond well in advance of threatened outbreaks and epidemics. With regard to the environment, they have agreed to coordinate positions in advance of future conferences on global problems such as climate change and biodiversity and have launched a joint initiative in the OECD aimed at reducing authorized levels of lead in fuel.

Under the third chapter of the Agenda on "Contributing to the Expansion of World Trade and Closer Economic Relations," the US and the EU have launched a joint study on ways to reduce or remove obstacles to transatlantic trade and investment. Although the leaders at the summit were unable to announce the conclusion of mutual recognition agreements in the telecommunications, pharmaceuticals, medical equipment and veterinary product sectors, as had been hoped, progress in these negotiations indicated that agreements could be reached by the end of 1996 or early 1997. Progress was also made on transatlantic negotiations in customs and veterinary agreements.

Under the fourth chapter of the Agenda on "Building Bridges Across the Atlantic," the US and the EU built on the TABD recommendations by holding a Transatlantic Automotive Industry Conference on international regulatory harmonization in Washington on 10-11 April 1995 under the sponsorship of the European Automobile Manufacturers Association (ACEA) and the Association of American Motor Vehicle Manufacturers (AAMA). Attended by business and government experts, the conference represents a major effort to minimize differences in the way the US and EU regulate automobile safety and emissions. The conference was motivated by two principal concerns: that the process of national or regional regulation does not correspond to the underlying economic reality that the motor vehicle industry is global, with the manufacture of components, assembly and sale frequently occurring on different continents; and that divergent standards substantially increase design and development costs, thereby raising prices to the detriment of the consumer.[2]

The conference sought to launch a process of global harmonization of regulations governing environmental standards (e.g. vehicle noise and emissions), safety standards (e.g. crash and theft protection) and testing procedures. The conference recommended that the US National Highway Transportation Safety Administration (NHTSA) accede to Working Party 29 of the United Nations Economic Commission for Europe (UN-ECE) in Geneva and that this body continue to serve as the focal point for international automotive harmonization efforts; in its report to the June US-EU summit in Washington, the Senior Level Group agreed to explore this possibility. The conference also recommended that the principle of mutual recognition of "functionally equivalent" standards should be applied whenever possible if harmonization could not be achieved, and that industry and government on both sides of the Atlantic should undertake joint or coordinated research programs. One of the central obstacles to these objectives, however, is the reluctance of national regulatory agencies, including the Environmental Protection Agency and the NHTSA in the US, to cede subject-matter jurisdiction.

As a follow-up to the inaugural Seville TABD conference, 15 issue groups were established to deal with a wide variety of horizontal and sectoral areas, such as standards, certification and regulatory policy; WTO implementation and expansion issues; trade liberalization; elimination of tariffs on information technology products; government procurement; intellectual property; international business practices; and investment and R&D.

In a Progress Report presented to the US and EU governments in late May 1996, the TABD Steering Committee highlighted the areas where progress had been reached since Seville. On standards, certification and regulatory policy, the report renewed calls made at Seville for MRAs in specific sectors; the acceptance of manufacturer's declaration as the rule, rather than the exception, with regard to product certification; greater transparency, participation and cooperation in standards setting, compliance requirements and product approvals and procedures; and greater use of functional standards in the setting of mandatory regulations. The report also called for renewed government commitment to support the multilateral process and the WTO; full implementation of Uruguay Round tariff cuts and the acceleration or increase of such cuts in those industrial sectors which have so requested; the identification and elimination of remaining national preferences in government procurement; the elaboration of a joint strategy to accelerate implementation of the Agreement on Trade Related aspects of Intellectual Property Rights (TRIPs) in newly industrialized and developing countries; implementation of the 1994 and 1996 OECD recommendations on illicit business practices; and support for the conclusion by Spring 1997 of the OECD negotiations on a Multilateral Agreement on Investments based on high standards. A follow-up conference of the TABD in Chicago on 8-9 November 1996 is expected to identify priorities for US-EU trade negotiations for approval at the December 1996 US-EU summit.

The US and EU also agreed to supplement the Transatlantic Business Dialogue with a Transatlantic Labor Dialogue between the AFL-CIO and the European Trade Union Confederation. Moreover, they have begun to implement a bilateral agreement on higher education and vocational training signed in December 1995 by EU Commissioner Edith Cresson and US Education Secretary Robert Reilly. According to this agreement, 60 educational and vocational establishments in 12 EU nations and 24 US states will be linked together in ten consortia, each composed of three institutions on each side of the Atlantic, on specific projects. For example, several establishments plan to offer jointly the first transatlantic masters program for graduate students interested in a career in public policy. It is envisaged that this program would also be offered on the information highway with interactive courses offered by faculties from universities on both sides of the Atlantic. It is also envisioned that joint study programs, followed by job placement and internships, will be offered in fields such as international business and health care.[3] Finally, the US and the EU announced at the June 1996 summit that they intended to sign a Science and Technology Agreement in 1997. This agreement will provide a legal framework for longstanding US-EU cooperation on research and may identify specific research projects on pressing transnational issues such as climate change.

The disappointments

Despite the positive notes sounded by the leaders at the summit and by the Senior Level Group's report to the summit, there was no denying that the "achievements" were, as one of the group's members remarked privately, "pretty thin gruel." Most disappointing, perhaps, was the failure of the US and the EU to achieve more to promote freer transatlantic and world trade, the most visible and concrete part of the Agenda.

The two sides were unable to conclude mutual recognition agreements in time for the June summit because they proved to be far more complex and problematic than had been anticipated. One of the main reasons for this was that progress toward concluding "second generation" agreements, covering both testing *and* certification, on telecommunications terminal equipment and other information technology products, electrical safety, electro-magnetic compatibility, pleasure boats and veterinary biologicals was held up by a dispute between the US and the EU over whether the conclusion of agreements in these areas should be linked to the conclusion of agreements on pharmaceuticals and medical devices. An MRA on pharmaceuticals will be particularly difficult to achieve: although the US Food and Drug Administration (FDA) may delegate the conduct of tests and the preparation of test reports according to Good Medical Practices, it does not have -- and is not seeking[4] -- legislative authority to delegate the certification of pharmaceutical products, except in certain circumstances. By contrast, the FDA may receive legislative authority to delegate certification of medical devices. Since the United States is very competitive in the European telecommunication and information technology market and Europe is competitive in the US pharmaceuticals market, the EU has sought to bundle the agreements together as a "package deal" to ensure that further opening of the former market is accompanied by opening of the latter market. The United States is eager to achieve progress where it is possible to do so on the ground that each agreement stands on its own merits.

The summit was also unable to register a target date for the completion of an Information Technology Agreement eliminating tariffs on high-technology products, such as telecommunications and computer products. Indeed, transatlantic disagreements about the future of the five-year bilateral US-Japan semiconductor agreement threatened the future of the agreement: the EU and Japan, on the one hand, were seeking a multilateralization of the agreement, the elimination of numerical targets, and EU participation in a new semiconductor forum even without prior EU tariff cuts in the sector; the United States, on the other hand, were seeking the renewal of the bilateral agreement, some protection of foreign chip makers' share of the Japanese market and a prior elimination of EU semiconductor tariffs.[5]

The US and the EU were also unable to satisfy their pledge in the Third Chapter of the Agenda to strengthen the multilateral trading system by working to complete unfinished business left over from the Uruguay Round, for example by concluding negotiations on the liberalization of telecommunications by the 30 April 1996 deadline and on liberalization of international maritime transport by the 30 June 1996 deadline. Unsatisfied with the offers on telecommunications from several countries, particularly the Asian "tigers," the United States withdrew from those negotiations and thereby forced their postponement until mid-February 1997. Whether this new deadline will be met will depend on whether improved offers will have been tabled by the time of the WTO Ministerial-level conference in Singapore in December 1996. The United States also withdrew from negotiations on the liberalization of financial services because of what it considered to be inadequate offers. There has been considerable criticism of the United States for taking a "free ride" on the results of the agreements reached through these negotiations: whereas it benefits from the concessions made by other countries as a signatory of the General Agreement on Trade in Services (GATS), it has taken a reservation on its own obligation to provide Most Favored Nation (MFN) treatment to other nations, thereby denying them the benefits of its own financial services regime. One week before the June 1996 US-EU summit, moreover, Washington announced that it would not submit an offer to deregulate its domestic shipping market and thereby forced a postponement of these negotiations until the next general round of negotiations on the liberalization of world trade in services to commence under WTO auspices in the year 2000.

Conflict over Cuba, Iran and Libya

In addition to the above set-backs,the June summit was overshadowed by serious transatlantic differences over US legislation aimed at penalizing companies doing business with Cuba, Libya and Iran.[6] Prompted by the shooting down by Cuban jets of two US civilian aircraft, killing four American citizens, over international air space in February 1996, Congress passed and President Clinton signed into law the Cuban Liberty and Democratic Solidarity (Libertad) Act (known as "the Helms-Burton Act" in honor of its primary sponsors) in order to tighten the economic embargo of Cuba. Providing for legal action against foreign companies and their executives who "traffic" in property formerly owned by US citizens, including Cuban exiles, and expropriated by Fidel Castro when he seized power in 1959, the Act contains a secondary boycott with clear extra-territorial effects. The Act enraged Washington's European allies (as well as Mexico and Canada), particularly those with investments in Cuba, which remain opposed to US efforts to legislate beyond its borders, critical of unilateral trade policies in violation of WTO obligations, and convinced that patient dialogue with and steady pressure on Cuba are more likely to achieve results than an embargo. During the press conference following the June summit, President Santer raised EU objections to the legislation in unusually blunt terms:

> This was not the Helms-Burton summit that some said it would be. But we did raise our concerns about the legislation in no uncertain terms with our American colleagues. The extraterritorial elements of this law have received worldwide condemnation. We are every bit as concerned about rogue states as the United States is. The European nations have fought terrorism at every opportunity, and will continue to do so. But this is a different issue. We do not believe that it is justifiable or effective for one country to impose its tactics on others and to threaten its friends while targeting its

adversaries. If that is done, it is bound to lead to reactions which it is in the interest of us both to avoid.

This statement surprised and annoyed some Administration officials because Santer had down-played the issue at the summit and had not given any indication that he would do otherwise at the press conference. The President defended the Act, but sounded a conciliatory note:

> I'm very sensitive to the whole question of extraterritoriality. We are reviewing that. But we think that the Cuban -- the persistent refusal of Cuba to move toward democracy or openness and the particular problems that causes for countries in our hemisphere and for the United States, especially, justified the passage of the bill, which I signed into law.

Questioned about the apparent contradiction between US condemnation of the Arab boycott of Israel and US willingness to impose a secondary boycott of its own against Cuba, President Clinton replied that the two were distinguishable: the Arab boycott was targeted against the *existence* of Israel, whereas the Helms-Burton Act was prompted by Cuba's actions in violation of international law; moreover, he noted that the Act provided him with flexibility in administration. This was a reference to his executive powers under the Act to grant a waiver of Title Three which enables American citizens to sue, in US courts, foreign companies or individuals who "traffic" in Cuban property expropriated from them.[7]

There was widespread awareness in the EU that, although the President was unenthusiastic about the Helms-Burton Act, he could not afford to alienate the Cuban-American communities in Florida and New Jersey, states whose electoral votes would play an important role in determining the outcome of the November presidential elections, or to give Republican challenger Bob Dole the opportunity to attack him for being "soft" on Castro. Nevertheless, the EU decided to make a strong public criticism of the Helms-Burton Act at the June summit in order to signal to the President that he should exercise his discretion to waive Title Three, to provide the President with a strong argument vis-à-vis Congress that US foreign policy interests would be damaged if he did not do so, and to signal to Congress not to pass pending legislation on Libya and Iran sponsored by Senator Alfonse D'Amato of New York.

The D'Amato Bill, signed into law by the President in August 1996, will require the President to impose certain sanctions -- including the denial of export licenses, denial of loans from financial institutions, a government buying ban, import restrictions and a prohibition on dealing in US financial instruments -- on companies making future investments which contribute directly and signficantly to the abilities of Iran and Libya to develop their petroleum resources. The EU was even more concerned about this legislation than the Helms-Burton Act: although the latter set a bad precedent for the extraterritorial imposition of US law, the EU's investment in Cuba is rather limited; by contrast, Iran and Libya together supply roughly 20 per cent of the EU's oil imports, the bulk of which is accounted for by Italy and Germany.

EU concerns were heightened when the House of Representatives unanimously passed its version of the D'Amato Bill on 19 June, albeit in a watered down form which reflected strong international condemnation of the original version. Convening at the European summit in Florence at the end of Italy's EU presidency, EU leaders issued a communiqué reiterating their opposition:

> The EU asserts its right and intention to react in defence of the EU's interest in respect to this legislation and any other secondary boycott legislation which has extra-territorial effects.[8]

The United States received the same message at the G-7 Lyon Summit of industrialized countries at the end of June; the communiqué from that conference referred to the obligation to "respect multilateral rules and principles."[9] The full court press continued through early July, with President Santer and EU ambassador to Washington Hugo Paemen sending letters of protest to President Clinton and Secretary Christopher, respectively.[10]

Delighted at the unusual unanimity of opinion within Europe, the even more unusual depth and speed of cooperation between the Commission and the member states,[11] and apparent success of European lobbying efforts to dilute the more objectionable aspects of the House of Representatives' version of the D'Amato Bill, the EU continued to press it case. On 16 July the White House announced that the President had decided to allow Title Three of the Helms-Burton Act to enter into force on 1 August 1996, but to postpone for six months -- from 1 August 1996 to 1 February 1997 -- the controversial right to file lawsuits against foreigners "trafficking" in confiscated property. The decision was hardly ideal: it created the legally uncertain situation that, although foreigners continuing to "traffic" in confiscated property after 1 November 1996 would be deemed as a matter of law to be causing injury, and therefore liable, to US nationals from whom the property had been seized, no right of action would exist against them until 1 February 1997 or some future time should the waiver be renewed. But the decision was an effort to steer a middle course between recognizing the legitimate grounds for objecting to the legislation, on the one hand, and recognizing the overwhelming support for the legislation in Congress and especially among the electorally important Cuban-American community, on the other. While recognizing the President's clear domestic political constraints and the fact that the right to sue under Title Three could be waived again by the President for further six month periods (which would be an easier political task following the November 1996 elections), the EU Commissioner Sir Leon Brittan nevertheless criticized the decision as a "welcome but limited step" which would keep a "sword of Damocles" hanging over the heads of European companies and individuals.

The EU began publicly to elaborate the counter-measures against Helms-Burton, and similar extra-territorial legislation, to which Santer referred at the summit: EU trade sanctions against the United States; an EU regulation binding in all Member States and/or Member State legislation preventing European companies from complying with the legislation and enabling them to counter-sue subsidiaries of US companies for damages awarded by US courts; Member State legislation imposing stricter visa and work permit regulations for US business executives; and/or a request that two-month long consultations be opened under WTO auspices, the first step toward the constitution of a dispute settlement panel should the dispute not be resolved amicably.[12]

Although many Europeans certainly thought that the United States had hoisted itself on its petard, many officials in the Administration felt with equal conviction that the EU had done so: as distasteful as they were and as incompatible with international law as they might be, the Helms-Burton Act and the D'Amato Bills were reactions to the inability or unwillingness of America's European allies to place serious pressure on Castro, the only non-democratic regime in the Western hemisphere, and to combat the scourge of international terrorism, primarily supported by Iran and Libya. In a written statement, the President warned the EU that the Administration would have difficulty showing further flexibility if Europe did not send a signal of greater resolution:

> The choice is clear: [The allies] can cease profiting from [American] property. They can join our efforts to promote a transition to democracy in Cuba. Or they can face the risk of full implementation [of the law].[13]

Senator D'Amato was rather less diplomatic:

> Our allies must understand that we must fight terrorism with action, not with platitudes. However, they seem to be more interested in profits than in closing down terrorist regimes.[14]

The Senator was not alone in his frustration. Senator Edward Kennedy, hardly known for his right-wing and isolationist or unilateralist views on foreign policy, introduced an amendment to the House of Representatives' version of the D'Amato Bill compelling, rather than entitling, the President to enforce sanctions on companies investing in Libya and Iran.[15] The explosion of a TWA jetliner off the US coast in mid-July 1996, and subsequent suspicions that that it may have been caused by a bomb planted by terrorists from the Middle East, only confirmed bipartisan support for cracking down on international terrorism. Six days after that explosion the House of Representatives passed the final bill unanimously.

Impatience with the EU's policies toward Cuba, Iran and Libya had been growing within the Administration and particularly in Congress on a bipartisan basis for already some time. Claims by the EU that it shares US desires for reform in Cuba have singularly failed to impress either branch about its seriousness of purpose: although the EU continues to exhort Cuba to open its markets and improve its human rights record, its words have not been accompanied by concrete actions. Even more seriously from Washington's perspective, the EU appears to be committed to a completely fruitless "critical dialogue" with Iran, which gives Teheran the impression that its relations with Europe can remain cordial regardless of its efforts to disrupt peace in the Middle East and support terrorism worldwide. Having undertaken the economically harmful step in 1995 of banning US oil companies from investing in Iran and from purchasing Iranian oil for sale to third countries, the Clinton Administration and Congress are particularly sensitive about Europe's continuing business relations with Iran and view the "critical dialogue" as a thinly veiled attempt to protect business interests, particularly German and French, rather than to encourage political reform there. The fact that French oil company Total has taken over a $600 million oil field development contract in Iran from which US oil company Conoco was compelled to withdraw has confirmed the view in the US that European companies are more than happy to profit from, and ultimately undermine, US sanctions against "rogue states."[16]

The Helms-Burton Act and the D'Amato Bill have seriously disturbed transatlantic harmony. But they have had an unintended and beneficial side-effect: the promotion of EU unity, an objective which the United States has often sought to promote! In an exceptional step, the embassies of the 15 EU member states in Washington closely coordinated their lobbying activities against this legislation through a specially composed task force. The discussion of the Helms-Burton Act and the D'Amato Bill in the General Affairs Council meeting of EU foreign ministers on 15 July 1996 was characterized by an unusual unanimity of opinion. It would be wrong, however, to conclude that the EU achieves its greatest degree of unity when it opposes the United States and that such unity will naturally cause transatlantic friction. While it is true that European unity may occasionally cause difficulties for the US, it will far more frequently promote US objectives. US-EU relations will occasionally suffer setbacks; but the process of increasingly strengthened transatlantic relations will continue because of the depth of common interests.

The longer-term prospects of the Agenda

This rather disappointing six-month interim report card is not the right yardstick by which to judge the New Transatlantic Agenda. It is far too soon to make definitive judgments about the Agenda's long-term impact on transatlantic relations. As noted above, several external factors slowed down progress under the Agenda during its first semester. Most significantly, the Helms-Burton and D'Amato Bills poisoned transatlantic relations, making long-standing differences of policy over Cuba, Iran and Libya even more contentious and holding up cooperation in many areas. Moreover, the first semester of the Agenda occurred during Italy's EU presidency, when Rome was distracted by national elections and compelled to devote its diplomatic resources to its primary responsibilities to the EU, such as launching the Inter-Governmental Conference.

Nevertheless, the long-term significance of the Agenda was already in evidence during the first half of 1996. Perhaps most important, the Agenda had led to a "widening" and "deepening" of contacts between US and EU officials. Before the launching of the Agenda, consultations remained focussed between a few institutional actors: Directorate-General I (External Economic Relations) of the European Commission and the Foreign Ministry of the EU presidency country, on the side of the EU, and the White House, the Department of State, the Department of Commerce and the Office of the US Trade Representative, on the side of the United States. Examples of the *wider contacts* encouraged by the Agenda include the cooperation between the US Department of Education and Directorate-General XXII (Human Resources, Education, Training and Youth) of the European Commission, leading to an agreement on higher education and vocational training signed in December 1995 between US Education Secretary Robert Reilly and EU Commissioner Edith Cresson, and the cooperation between the US Department of Labor and Directorate-General V (Employment, Industrial Relations and Social Affairs) of the European Commission, leading to a memorandum of understanding signed between Secretary of Labor Robert Reich and EU Commissioner Padraig Flynn launching a US-EU Working Group on Labor and Employment Issues. This "widening" of transatlantic contacts is particularly significant because it will enrich the dialogue and create new constituencies for US-EU cooperation.

The Agenda has also led to more contacts at *lower levels* than had previously been the case. In addition to the traditional meetings at the head of state, ministerial and trade negotiator levels, the Agenda has generated regular meetings in the Senior Level Group between Under-Secretaries and Political Directors and between mid-level officials who do the large bulk of the day-to-day work set forth in the Agenda.

The Agenda has altered the *tone and substance* of transatlantic contacts. In its report to the June 1996 summit, the Senior Level Group reported that "a new spirit of cooperation and commitment to joint action pervades the relationship." This was not simply public relations. As has been noted above, before the launching of the Agenda in December 1995, transatlantic consultations have tended to be briefing sessions given by US officials for their European counterparts, with little substantive dialogue and even less follow-up. By engaging both the US and the EU in a common enterprise of long-term perspective and broad scope, the Agenda has generated a true exchange of views and has strengthened the reflexes of officials to think in terms of transatlantic, rather than purely national, interests and objectives.

The Agenda has vastly increased the *range of areas* for transatlantic cooperation. Whereas transatlantic consultations used to be focussed principally on contentious issues of bilateral trade, the issues on which the United States and EU are pledged to take joint action cover a vast spectrum -- security, international trade, the environment, science, health, education and humanitarian assistance and development, to name just a few. These issues are noteworthy because they are of *global* rather than just *transatlantic* interest. Moreover, some of the regions of the world toward which the United States and the EU have pledged to coordinate their foreign policies -- such as the Middle East and Russia -- are noteworthy because they have often been the source of serious transatlantic disputes in the past. The United States and Europe have often pursued divergent policies with regard to the Arab-Israeli conflict and Russia; at certain moments, including during the Yom Kippur War and President Reagan's effort to impose sanctions on European companies participating in the construction of the Siberian pipeline, these divergences have severely strained the transatlantic relationship. Many of the other regions of the world toward which the United States and the EU have pledged in the Agenda to coordinate their foreign policies -- such as Central America, the Caribbean and the Horn of Africa -- have never previously been the source of systematic transatlantic cooperation.

Finally, unlike the 1990 Transatlantic Declaration and other US-EU agreements, the Agenda was conceived as a *flexible document* whose Action Plan would be regularly modified at every US-EU summit to reflect progress that has been achieved since the prior summit, the current context of transatlantic relations and different priorities for action in the future. The flexibility of the Agenda, coupled with the task of the Senior Level Group to monitor US-EU relations and to update and revise priorities in the Agenda for consideration at the semi-annual summits, enable the US and EU to devote as much attention to *conflict prevention* through 'early warning' as to conflict resolution. It may therefore succeed in taking US-EU relations well beyond the sterile model of *ad hoc* summit meetings and make transatlantic relations more responsive to changing concerns and events -- as well as more immediately relevant to the lives of individuals -- in Europe and the United States.

Notes

1   See Press Conference by President Clinton, President Santer of the European Commission and Prime Minister Prodi of Italy and New Transatlantic Agenda Senior Level Group Report to the US-EU Summit, in USIA Wireless File, 13 June 1996, pp. 19-25; Elizabeth Wise, "Clouds Loom Over EU-US Talks," *European Voice*, 6-12 June 1996, at p. 9; *Agence Europe*, No. 6746, 12 June 1996, at p. 4; and *European Report*, No. 2139, 12 June 1996, at V.7-8.

2   According to a report released at the conference, differences between Europe and the United States in the design and development cost of motor vehicles amount to about 10 per cent of the final cost of certain models of passenger cars.

3   Elizabeth Wise, "Progress on Plans For Transatlantic Degree," *European Voice*, 6-12 June 1996.

4   There is great sensitivity on the part of the Food and Drug Administration (FDA) to relinquish its power of certifying pharmaceuticals and medical devices, largely because of the enormous legal liability attaching to the sale of faulty products in the United States.

5   Guy de Jonquières, "Japan Takes Tougher Line In Chips Dispute With US," *The Financial Times*, 1 July 1996.

6   Captured the prevailing sentiment in Europe, one journalist slammed America's "high-handed, dictatorial behavior" and claimed that "the United States has been acting as if it alone were entitled to dictate the terms of world trade, apparently on the grounds that -- at least in a presidential election year -- American interests take priority over

everyone else's." Reginald Dale, "America's Bullying Trade Tactics," *International Herald Tribune*, 11 June 1996.

7   By contrast, the President does not have the power to waive Title Four, which restricts entry into the US of senior executives, major shareholders, and "agents" such as lawyers or accountants, along with their families, of companies which "traffic" in expropriated property.

8   Quoted in Lionel Barber, "EU Summit Warns US on Sanctions," *The Financial Times*, 24 June 1996.

9   *Agence Europe*, No. 6760, 29 June 1996.

10   Alan Friedman, "Allies Press U.S. To Back Down On Cuba Sanctions," *International Herald Tribune*, 12 July 1996. In his letter to Clinton, President Santer invoked the spirit of the New Transatlantic Agenda and intimated that the Helms-Burton Act was incompatible with efforts to deepen the transatlantic partnership. See *Europe*, No. 6770, 13 July 1996.

11   Following a General Affairs Council meeting of EU foreign ministers, Sir Leon Brittan declared, with characteristic British understatement: "I was frankly surprised at the unanimity of their conclusions, the rapidity of their deliberations and the determination of their action." As quoted in *European Report*, 16 July 1996.

12   As President Santer had presumably been informed by the Commission's Legal Service, however, that bringing a case against the United States before the WTO would be problematic: Washington could argue that legitimate national security concerns justify the embargo; moreover, European trade with Cuba is not injured because it is largely in the form of investments, rather than goods, and WTO rules on the former are still not fully in place. The EU could legally impose trade sanctions, however, in areas such as aviation, maritime transport and telecommunications services which are not yet explicitly covered by the WTO's Most Favored Nation principle, prohibiting discrimination between trade partners.

13   As quoted in "Clinton Puts Cuba Lawsuits on Hold," *The Wall Street Journal* (European Edition), 17 July 1996.

14   As quoted in "US Faces Fresh Dispute Over Sanctions," *The The Financial Times*, 18 July 1996.

15   In the version of the bill which finally passed, the President retains discretion to waive the application of sanctions under certain circumstances.

16   Indeed, one of the reasons why France lobbied hard to lift United
       Nations sanctions on Iraq as soon as possible, even while the UN
       Security Council Observer Mission (UNSCOM) warned of
       continued efforts by Iraq to develop weapons of mass destruction,
       was that Total and Elf Acquitaine had signed massive oil field
       development contracts there which would take effect once sanctions
       were lifted. To some observers within the Administration it appears
       as if the EU is prepared to go to extraordinary lengths to get along
       with Teheran in order to protect such business interests: rather than
       demand that the *fatwa* (death sentence) against British author
       Salman Rushdie be officially lifted, for example, the EU offered at
       one stage to accept it on condition that Teheran secretly pledge not
       to carry it out.

9 Conclusions

With the Clinton Administration, the wheel has come full circle, back to a brand of pro-Community policies which characterized the Truman, Eisenhower and Kennedy Administrations. As in the 1950s and early 1960s, the Administration's EU policy is born of the conviction that continued integration is good for Europe, good for the United States and good for the stability of those regions which border on the EU. In several respects, however, the Clinton Administration's policy toward the EU is unique: it is partly motivated by the belief that a strong EU will enhance transatlantic cooperation on a wide variety of global issues; it has actively encouraged the development of a European security and defense identity, complementing the role of NATO, on the ground that this development will strengthen transatlantic security; and, in distinction to prior administrations' EU policies which engaged in ritual invocations of a transatlantic 'partnership,' this Administration's policy has focussed on taking active steps through the joint actions of the New Transatlantic Agenda to make that partnership a reality.

Apart from the areas of trade and foreign aid, there clearly will be limits to this partnership. The EU's Common Foreign and Security Policy promises to be little more than a weak instrument in the near future. In the military and security field, NATO is likely to remain the only collective defense organization in the West capable of dealing with serious conflict. Through its recent intervention in Bosnia, NATO has demonstrated that it has not outlived its usefulness after the end of the Cold War; it will remain an essential means of responding to security threats to the Alliance from outside the North Atlantic and European area, and perhaps even against a nationalistic and militaristic Russia.

But the United States seeks a strengthened partnership with the EU because it sees the latter as a natural ally on many issues, especially in liberalizing markets and trade, stabilizing the former Soviet Bloc, the Third World, and addressing many global environmental, humanitarian and security challenges.

The New Transatlantic Agenda recognizes that the traditional dividing line between foreign and domestic policy will be increasingly blurred in the post-Cold War world and that the future is likely to bring a host of new global challenges which will demand a coordinated transatlantic response of a non-military nature. These challenges include:

- Economic and political upheavals in the Third World resulting from overpopulation, poverty, famine or disease; in seeking to stabilize the Third World and prevent massive migration toward their affluent societies, the US and the EU will be essential partners in providing economic, technical and humanitarian assistance.

- Proliferation of weapons of mass destruction, particularly the acquisition of nuclear, chemical and biological weapons by pariah states, such as Iran, Iraq, Libya and North Korea; in seeking to improve controls over the raw materials and the scientific knowledge related to the production of such weapons, the US and the EU will be essential partners in ensuring the effectiveness of the New Forum, the successor to the Coordinating Committee on Export Controls (COCOM), and the Non-Proliferation Treaty.

- Environmental degradation and depletion of natural and mineral resources; in seeking to reduce CO_2 emissions and global warming, replenish rapidly diminishing fish stocks, and conserve water, the US and the EU will be essential partners in the goal to develop cleaner factories and means of transportation, more efficient recycling programs, and safer treatment of hazardous wastes, as well as to encourage developing countries to adopt family planning policies and sustainable development programs.

- High unemployment, crime, drug addiction, and the disintegration of the family structure; in seeking to reduce stubbornly high unemployment in the EU and stagnant wages and lack of job security in the US, both sides must work together to stimulate economic growth through freer transatlantic and world trade.

The limits on the competence of the EU, particularly the European Commission, will naturally require the United States to maintain an active dialogue with the Member States to make progress on these issues. The Inter-Governmental Conference will determine in large part whether EU institutions and decision-making procedures will be streamlined and whether the EU will become a more coherent actor on the world stage. But transatlantic cooperation within the framework of the Agenda will also play a significant role in determining whether the European Commission's competence expands in many areas. Such a result would be generally welcomed in Washington: the United States frequently finds cooperation with the EU to be easier than with its Member States because the former has a pan-European or international, rather than a state-centric, perspective. Unlike France, moreover, the EU does not have the reflex of an influential country seeking to display its independence by defining positions which are contrary to, or distinct from, those of the United States.

Global challenges, such as those outlined above, obviously cannot be addressed if the United States and the European Union do not have sufficient economic resources at their disposal. Such resources can only be generated through economic growth, in which the liberalization of international trade will play an important part.

Washington finds in the European Commission a valuable ally against the protectionist excesses and support for state intervention in certain Member States. The Commission, supported by the European Court of Justice, has played a key role in ensuring that Europe has moved toward a single market and the Anglo-Saxon model of a liberal market economy, rather than the *dirigiste* model and national industrial policies still popular in several Member States. The fact that the European economy is still suffocated by overly generous welfare and labor legislation, including at the EU level, is largely the result of Member State initiatives over which the Commission has had no control or Member State pressure on the Commission to adopt particular legislation. As European unemployment continues to climb and European industry continues to lose competitiveness vis-à-vis its American and Asian competitors, the need to move further toward the Anglo-Saxon model, including deregulation, privatization and greater flexibility in the labor markets, is becoming increasingly apparent. Although the Commission has adopted a low profile in response to the backlash against further progress toward economic and political union after Maastricht, its influence is likely to rise anew because it is the institution which must logically lead the process of perfecting market integration and promoting the economic liberalization upon which Europe's growth and prosperity depend.

Notwithstanding high growth rates in Asia and rapidly expanding trade between the US and the Pacific Rim, the transatlantic trade relationship remains of primary importance and further steps to liberalize that trade still promise significant rewards. As the scale of transatlantic trade is already so large, with two-way trade in goods and services worth roughly $250 billion in 1994, even small increases in this trade would yield huge new export markets: if average annual US and EU domestic growth rates were 3 per cent, transatlantic exports would more than double over the next ten years.[1]

While the United States runs increasingly large deficits with Asia and sells primarily raw materials in exchange for manufactured and high-technology goods, transatlantic trade is balanced both in terms of the value and nature of the goods exchanged. US and European deficits with Asia persist, despite the decline of their currencies against the yen, because of structural and hidden barriers to importation; transatlantic trade, by contrast, remains in overall balance through macro-economic management.

Most importantly, the total stock of Foreign Direct Investment (FDI) which Europe and the US have in each other dwarfs that which either has with Asia: about 41 per cent of all US FDI abroad is in Europe and roughly 54 per cent of all FDI in the US is of European origin.[2] The nature of the investments exchanged across the Atlantic are also profoundly different from those exchanged across the Pacific. The United States and Europe invest more in research and development in each other and exchange more technology than they do with Asia. The investments they make in each other yield greater profits than those they make in Asia; the investments they receive from each other yield higher paying jobs and tax revenues than those from Asia.[3] The scope and nature of foreign direct investment are more important indicators of interdependence than bilateral trade: whereas trade can be conducted at a distance, FDI usually implies a stake in, and commitment to, the host country. As the United States and Europe have a growing stake in the economic health of the other, each has significant incentives to pursue policies in cooperation with the other, rather than to pursue zero-sum economic strategies. The trans-Pacific trade relationship is more prone to conflict than the transatlantic one because it is not characterized by this degree of interdependence.

In general, the transatlantic business community has a particularly strong interest in strengthening this interdependence. Just as the European business community served as the principal motor of European integration, the transatlantic business community will serve as the principal motor of transatlantic integration. As in the past, many of the decisions which businesses take on a day-to-day basis -- regarding investments, trade and cooperative linkages -- will continue to shape the economic context for political decisions. In an important new development, however, the Transatlantic Business Dialogue offers US and European businesses a structured forum in which to elaborate and communicate to Washington and Brussels a set of priorities for further trade and investment liberalization, not only across the Atlantic but in third markets as well. Private associations of business and political leaders, such as the Transatlantic Policy Network, will also continue to play a critical role in promoting transatlantic linkages and in fostering further initiatives for US-EU joint actions.

While US-EU trade disputes are not infrequent or unimportant, the considerable attention paid to them exaggerates their seriousness compared to the large volume of transatlantic trade and investment. Indeed, these disputes tend to mask the underlying truth that Europeans and Americans have a strong commonality of views about the future of the world economic order:

> Although there are clear differences between American capitalism and European capitalism, they are dwarfed in comparison with the gulf existing across the Pacific. If the United States is to influence significantly the rapidly emerging global economy, it will need allies. Many of these allies are to be found within Europe.[4]

The US and the EU have been essential partners in bringing every round of GATT negotiations, including the Uruguay Round, to a successful conclusion. Similarly, further negotiations to liberalize world trade will require transatlantic partnership. Largely as a result of the European Commission's efforts to reinforce the role of free competition as the guarantor of the single market, the European Union's economic organization and outlook toward international trade are remarkably similar to those of the United States. In order to ensure a liberal international trading order and protect the viability of their own economic systems, the US and the EU will need to cooperate in responding to the challenges of the Asian economic model. This will particularly be the case in presenting joint complaints before the WTO and in collaborating closely on the terms of China's WTO accession.

The United States and the European Union would do well to remember that "The multilateral trade system is really the trilateral trade system: if you can get an ally on an issue, you win 2-1."[5] By focussing on day-to-day transatlantic disputes, rather than on unfair trade practices around the world, particularly in Asia, both sides seriously damage their own interests. In order to work effectively together to strengthen the discipline of free and fair competition, the US must resist the temptation of "going it alone" by cutting separate deals which exclude the EU, and the EU must resist the temptation of standing aside while the US assumes the burden of negotiating freer access for all to world markets.

In particular, it was a mistake for the United States to exclude the EU from its bilateral agreements with Japan to ensure access by foreign semiconductor manafacturers to the Japanese market and to monitor the purchase of foreign-made car parts by Japanese motor vehicle manufacturers. Fortunately, at the time this book went to press, the US had signalled that the EU was welcome to join a follow-on semiconductor agreement (albeit on condition that the latter gave its prior commitment to signing an Information Technology Agreement eliminating transatlantic tariffs on information technology products) and that the EU was also welcome to participate as a member, rather than merely as an observer, in September 1996 discussions with Japan regarding purchases of car parts.

The EU has frequently criticized Washington's high-pressure tactics in trade negotiations and claimed that they reflect a preference for "managed trade" rather than a multilateral trading regime based on rules enforced by the WTO. These charges overlook the Clinton Administration's commitment to the latter, evinced by the campaign to ensure Congressional ratification of the Uruguay Round Agreements and NAFTA and in the US record of bringing cases to and complying with judgments of the WTO. The charges also overlook the fact that the results-oriented trade diplomacy of the US has done far more to advance open markets and free and fair trade than the EU's discrete approach. Although the EU has recently toughened its trade policies vis-à-vis Japan, China and the Asian "tigers," its frequent criticisms of US trade policy, coupled with its eagerness to benefit from the results thereof, have annoyed many leading officials within the Administration and have unfortunately confirmed the view of many isolationists and "unilateralists" within Congress that the EU is a "free-rider" on US efforts to promote free and fair trade, as well as to preserve peace and promote democracy, around the globe.

Transatlantic cooperation is clearly damaged when the United States applies its laws extraterritorially on its allies, as in the Helms-Burton Act and the D'Amato Bill, in violation of international law, US commitments under the WTO, and commitments in the New Transatlantic Agenda to strengthen the multilateral trading system. The EU's high-profile campaign against both pieces of legislation in mid-1996 failed to appreciate, however, the difficult position of the Administration in a presidential election year, the impact on American public opinion of international terrorist attacks against US targets, and the fact that the

108

EU's timidity in dealing with the Castro regime and world terrorism, sponsored largely by Iran and Libya, had partly motivated the legislation.

Although the Administration had little enthusiasm for Helms-Burton, there was overwhelming bipartisan support for it in both houses of Congress and sufficient votes to override a presidential veto. The shooting down of American planes over international waters by Cuban jets was, of course, an important reason for this support; but the perception that the EU was paying lip-service to human rights while strengthening its trade and political links with Cuba, thereby securing Castro's hold on power, was also significant because it reinforced the conviction in Congress that the legislation had to be applied extra-territorially. Compared to the D'Amato Bill, however, Helms-Burton presents limited risks for long-lasting strains in the transatlantic relationship. President Clinton exercised the discretion given to him under Helms-Burton to waive the right of Americans to bring suit in US courts for six months and it may be that, without the distraction of electoral concerns, this right will be postponed for subsequent six-months periods. EU Member States could strengthen the President's case for doing so by agreeing to a pro-democracy code of conduct for foreign investors, such as the one which existed in South Africa under *apartheid*.

The D'Amato Bill presents a more serious risk to transatlantic relations than the Helms-Burton Act. Even though the mere *threat* of sanctions under Helms-Burton has already convinced certain European companies to restrict or terminate their activities in Cuba, European investment -- with the exception of Spanish investment in the tourism sector -- has been limited to date and has modest potential in the future. By contrast, the D'Amato Bill targets future investments in the energy sector in Iran and Libya on which Europe depends for secure energy supplies. But the D'Amato Bill, like the Helms-Burton Act, allows the President considerable flexibility in implementation: he may waive the application of sanctions if he determines that it is important to the national interest to do so and may delay imposing sanctions while consulting with foreign governments in an effort to terminate sanctionable activities. With regard to Iran, the President may waive imposition of sanctions against nationals of countries taking "significant action" to increase political and economic pressure on that country. Although the meaning of this phrase is uncertain, it may well be elastic enough to cover actions by EU Member States to prevent their oil companies from carrying out projects in Iran from which US firms, such as Conoco, have been compelled to withdraw. With regard to both Iran and Libya, the President would have a case for waiving sanctions if EU Member States took the rather modest steps of denying export credits or risk insurance to companies investing there.

The reasons why this legislation enjoyed overwhelming support in Congress, and was signed into law by the President, may be traced to the traumatic experience of the United States with the seizure of American hostages in 1979 during the Iranian Revolution, the destruction of a Pan Am jetliner over Scotland by a Libyan bomb in 1980 and, more recently, to suspicions that Iran and/or Libya were behind Hizbullah's devastating campaign of terror on the streets of Israel to derail the Middle East peace process, the explosion of an American military apartment complex in Dhahran, Saudi Arabia, and the destruction of a TWA airliner near Long Island in mid-1996. The bomb explosions at the World Trade Center in 1993, the Alfred P. Murrah Federal Building in Oklahoma City in 1995, and in Atlanta during the Olympic Games in 1996 have also served to heighten the American public's sensitivity to the issue of terrorism, whether it be international or home-grown. While Europe has certainly suffered more than its share of terrorist attacks, its geographical position and history of conflict have forced its public to come to terms with its own vulnerability. By contrast, terrorist attacks against American targets abroad, and in particular on US territory, generate shock because they shatter the myth of America's invulnerability or capacity to remain isolated from world events. Although this may not justify passage of the D'Amato Bill, it explains the overwhelming bipartisan support for it in the United States and the conviction that, in light of the EU's apparent reluctance to place serious political and economic pressure on Teheran and Tripoli, sanctions had to be imposed extra-territorially.

The frictions caused by the Helms-Burton Act and the D'Amato Bill are not likely to disappear after the November 1996 presidential elections: it is uncertain whether the new Congress will have different views with regard to this legislation; despite some room for maneuver, the Clinton Administration will have no choice but to apply the law; and it is uncertain whether EU Member States will take sufficient action to convince President Clinton to waive sanctions or Congress to repeal the legislation. There will need to be movement on both sides to defuse the tensions generated by this legislation: while seeking its eventual repeal by Congress, the Administration should exercise maximum restraint in its application; as for the EU, it should wait to see how the legislation is applied in practice, rather than continue its vociferous condemnation of it, and should help the President exercise the discretion which he enjoys under the legislation by indicating its willingness to be serious about encouraging democracy in Cuba and placing pressure on Iran and Libya to terminate their sponsorship of terrorism.

Both the US and the EU need to bear in mind that their relationship is and will remain central to the key economic and political challenges facing both sides of the Atlantic into the next century. The New Transatlantic Agenda has charted the course for a more effective transatlantic partnership to cope more effectively with those challenges. Progress under the Agenda toward closer

US-EU relations will not always be linear or rapid; occasional disputes will continue to arise. But by keeping such transitory issues which divide them in the perspective of those wider, more significant and enduring interests which bind them together, the US and the EU will be more likely to fulfil the great promise contained in the Agenda.

Notes

1   Commission MEMO/95/163. From the perspective of the United States, the resulting increase in the size of the European market would be equivalent to the entire Taiwan market, the eighth largest export market for the United States. Even a one per cent increase in exports to Europe would create 20,000 new US jobs; many of the jobs created by such exports are concentrated in high-technology sectors and tend to be high-paying. Moreover, jobs created by European firms in the US pay 18 per cent more on average than other US jobs.

2   US Department of Commerce, Survey of Current Business, August 1995. Total transatlantic investment amounts to around $460 billion. US direct investment in Europe is roughly $250 billion, compared with only $48 billion in all of Asia. Glennon Harrison, *CRS Report for Congress: US-European Union Trade and Investment*, Congressional Research Service, The Library of Congress, 20 December 1994, p. 8 of summary.

3   Robin Gaster and Clyde Prestowitz Jr., "Shrinking the Atlantic: Europe and the American Economy," North Atlantic Research, Inc. and the Economic Strategy Institute, 1995. Roughly three million US workers are employed by European-owned companies.

4   Robin Gaster and Clyde Prestowitz Jr., "Shrinking the Atlantic: Europe and the American Economy," North Atlantic Research, Inc. and the Economic Strategy Institute, 1995, p. 61.

5   Japanese diplomat, quoted in Tom Buerkle, "Fair Play? It's a Trilateral Trade World," *International Herald Tribune*, 28 June 1996.

Appendix I

The New Transatlantic Agenda and Action Plan

We, the United States of America and the European Union, affirm our conviction that the ties which bind our people are as strong today as they have been for the past half century. For over fifty years, the transatlantic partnership has been the leading force for peace and prosperity for ourselves and for the world. Together, we helped transform adversaries into allies and dictatorships into democracies. Together, we built institutions and patterns of cooperation that ensured our security and economic strength. These are epic achievements.

Today we face new challenges at home and abroad. To meet them, we must further strengthen and adapt the partnership that has served us so well. Domestic challenges are not an excuse to turn inward; we can learn from each other's experiences and build new transatlantic bridges. We must first of all seize the opportunity presented by Europe's historic transformation to consolidate democracy and free-market economies throughout the continent.

We share a common strategic vision of Europe's future security. Together, we have charted a course for ensuring continuing peace in Europe into the next century. We are committed to the construction of a new European security architecture in which the North Atlantic Treaty Organisation, the European Union, the Western European Union, the Organisation for Security and Cooperation in Europe and the Council of Europe have complementary and mutually reinforcing roles to play.

We reaffirm the indivisibility of transatlantic security. NATO remains, for its members, the centrepiece of transatlantic security, providing the indispensable link between North America and Europe. Further adaptation of the Alliance's political and military structures to reflect both the full spectrum of its roles and the development of the emerging European Security and Defence Identity will strengthen the European pillar of the Alliance.

As to the accession of new members to NATO and to the EU, these processes, autonomous but complementary, should contribute significantly to the extension of security, stability and prosperity in the whole of Europe. Furthering the work of Partnership for Peace and the North Atlantic Cooperation Council and establishing a security partnership between NATO and Russia and between NATO and Ukraine will lead to unprecedented cooperation on security issues.

We are strengthening the OSCE so that it can fulfil its potential to prevent destabilising regional conflicts and advance the prospect of peace, security, prosperity and democracy for all.

Increasingly, our common security is further enhanced by strengthening and reaffirming the ties between the European Union and the United States within the existing network of relationships which join us together.

Our economic relationship sustains our security and increases our prosperity. We share the largest two-way trade and investment relationship in the world. We bear a special responsibility to lead multilateral efforts towards a more open world system of trade and investment. Our cooperation has made possible every global trade agreement, from the Kennedy Round to the Uruguay Round. Through the G-7, the work to stimulate global growth. And at the Organisation for Economic Cooperation and Development, we are developing strategies to overcome structural unemployment and adapt to demographic change.

We are determined to create a New Transatlantic Marketplace, which will expand trade and investment opportunities and multiply jobs on both sides of the Atlantic. This initiative will also contribute to the dynamism of the global economy.

At the threshold of a new century, there is a new world to shape - full of opportunities but with challenges no less critical than those faced by previous generations. These challenges can be met and opportunities fully realised only by the whole international community working together. We will work with others bilaterally, at the United Nations and in other multilateral fora.

We are determined to reinforce our political and economic partnership as a powerful force for good in the world. To this end, we will build on the extensive consultations established by the 1990 Transatlantic Declaration and the conclusions of our June 1995 Summit and move to common action.

Today we adopt a **New Transatlantic Agenda** based on a Framework for Action with four major goals:

Promoting peace and stability, democracy and development around the world

Together, we will work for an increasingly stable and prosperous Europe; foster democracy and economic reform in Central and Eastern Europe as well as in Russia, Ukraine and other new independent states; secure peace in the Middle East; advance human rights; promote non-proliferation and cooperate on development and humanitarian assistance.

Responding to global challenges

Together, we will fight international crime, drug-trafficking and terrorism; address the needs of refugees and displaced persons; protect the environment and combat disease.

Contributing to the expansion of world trade and closer economic relations

Together, we will strengthen the multilateral trading system and take concrete, practical steps to promote closer economic relations between us.

Building bridges across the Atlantic

Together, we will work with our business people, scientists, educators and others to improve communication and to ensure that future generations remain as committed as we are to developing a full and equal partnership.

Within this Framework, we have developed an extensive **Joint EU-US Action Plan**. We will give special priority between now and our next Summit to the following actions:

I PROMOTING PEACE AND STABILITY, DEMOCRACY AND DEVELOPMENT AROUND THE WORLD

- We pledge to work boldly and rapidly, together and with other partners, to implement the peace, to assist recovery of the war-ravaged regions in the former Yugoslavia and to support economic and political reform and new democratic institutions. We will cooperate to ensure: (1) respect for human rights, for the rights of minorities and for the rights of refugees and displaced persons, in particular the right of return; (2) respect for the work of the War Crimes Tribunal, established by the United Nations Security Council in order to ensure international criminal accountability; (3) the establishment of a framework for free and fair elections in Bosnia-Herzegovina as soon as conditions permit and (4) the implementation of the agreed process for arms controls, disarmament and confidence-building measures. While continuing to provide humanitarian assistance, we will contribute to the task of reconstruction, subject to the implementation of the provisions of the peace settlement plan, in the context of the widest possible burden-sharing with other donors and taking advantage of the experience of international institutions, of the European Commission and of all relevant bilateral donors in the coordination mechanism.
- We will support the countries of Central and Eastern Europe in their efforts to restructure their economies and strengthen their democratic and market institutions. Their commitment to democratic systems of government, respect of minorities, human rights, market oriented economies and good relations with neighbours will facilitate their integration into our institutions. We are taking steps to intensify our cooperation aimed at sharing information, coordinating and securing the safety of their nuclear power stations.
- We are determined to reinforce our cooperation to consolidate democracy and stability in Russia, Ukraine and other new independent states. We are committed to working with them in strengthening democratic institutions and market reforms, in protecting the environment, in securing the safety of their nuclear power stations and in promoting their integration into the international economy. An enduring and stable security framework for Europe must include these nations. We intend to continue building a close partnership with a democratic Russia. An independent, democratic, stable and nuclear weapons-free Ukraine will contribute to security and stability in Europe; we will cooperate to support Ukraine's democratic and economic reforms.

- We will support the Turkish Government's efforts to strengthen democracy and advance economic reforms in order to promote Turkey's further integration into the transatlantic community.
- We will work towards a resolution of the Cyprus question, taking into account the prospective accession of Cyprus to the European Union. We will support the UN Secretary General's Mission of Good Offices and encourage dialogue between and with the Cypriot communities.
- We reaffirm our commitment to the achievement of a just, lasting and comprehensive peace in the Middle East. We will build on the recent successes in the Peace Process, including the bold steps taken by Jordan and Israel, through concerted efforts to support agreements already concluded and to expand the circle of peace. Noting the important milestone reached with the signing of the Palestinian Interim Agreement, we will play an active role at the Conference for Economic Assistance to the Palestinians, will support the regional parties in implementing the conclusions of the Amman Summit. We will also continue our efforts to promote peace between Israel, Lebanon and Syria. We will actively seek the dismantling of the Arab boycott of Israel.
- We pledge to work together more closely in our preventive and crisis diplomacy; to respond effectively to humanitarian emergencies; to promote sustainable development and the building of democratic societies; and to support human rights.
- We have agreed to coordinate, cooperate and act jointly in devilment and humanitarian assistance activities. To this end, we will establish a High-Level Consultative Group to review progress of existing efforts, to assess policies and priorities and to identify projects and regions for the further strengthening of cooperation.
- We will increase in developing a blueprint for UN economic and social reform. We will cooperate to find urgently needed solutions to the financial crisis of the UN system. We are determined to keep our commitments, including our financial obligations. At the same time, the UN must direct its resources to the highest priorities and must reform in order to meet its fundamental goals.
- We will provide support to the Korean Peninsula Energy Development Organisation (KEDO), underscoring our shared desire to resolve important proliferation challenges throughout the world.

II   RESPONDING TO GLOBAL CHALLENGES

- We are determined to take new steps in our common battle against the scourges of international crime, drug trafficking and terrorism. We commit ourselves to active, practical cooperation between the US and the future European Police Office, EUROPOL. We will jointly support and contribute to ongoing training programmes and institutions for crime-fighting officials in Central and Eastern Europe, Russia, Ukraine, other new independent states and other parts of the globe.
- We will work together to strengthen multilateral efforts to protect the global environment and to develop environmental policy strategies for sustainable world-wide growth. We will coordinate our negotiating positions on major global environmental issues, such as climate change, ozone layer depletion, persistent organic pollutants, desertification and erosion and contaminated soils. We are undertaking coordinated initiatives to disseminate environmental technologies and to reduce the public health risks from hazardous substances, in particular from exposure to lead. We will strengthen our bilateral cooperation on chemicals, biotechnology and air pollution issues.
- We are committed to develop and implement an effective global early warning system and response network for new and re-emerging communicable diseases such as AIDS and the Ebola virus, and to increase training and professional exchanges in this area. Together, we call on other nations to join us in more effectively combating such diseases.

III   CONTRIBUTION TO THE EXPANSION OF WORLD TRADE AND CLOSER ECONOMIC RELATIONS

- We have a special responsibility to strengthen the multilateral trading system, to support the World Trade Organisation and to lead the way in opening markets to trade and investment.
- We will contribute to the expansion of world trade by fully implementing our Uruguay Round commitments, work for the completion of the unfinished business by the agreed timetables and encourage a successful and substantive outcome for the Singapore WTO Ministerial Meeting in December 1996. In this context we will explore the possibility of agreeing on a mutually satisfactory package of tariff reductions on industrial products, and we will consider which, if any, Uruguay Round obligations on tariffs can be implemented on an

accelerated basis. In view of the importance of the information society, we are launching a specific exercise in order to attempt to conclude an information technology agreement.

- We will work together for the successful conclusion of a Multilateral Agreement on Investment at the OECD that espouses strong principles on international investment liberalisation and protection. Meanwhile, we will work to develop discussion of the issue with our partners at the WTO. We will address in appropriate fora problems where trade intersects with concerns for the environment, internationally recognised labour standards and competition policy. We will cooperate in creating additional trading opportunities, bilaterally and throughout he world, in conformity with our WTO commitments.
- Without detracting from our cooperation in multilateral fora, we will create a New Transatlantic Marketplace by progressively reducing or eliminating barriers that hinder the flow of goods, services and capital between us. We will carry out a joint study on ways of facilitating trade in goods and services and further reducing or eliminating tariff and non-tariff barriers.
- We will strengthen regulatory cooperation, in particular by encouraging regulatory agencies to give a high priority to cooperation with their respective transatlantic counterparts, so as to address technical and non-tariff barriers to trade resulting from divergent regulatory processes. We aim to conclude an agreement on mutual recognition of conformity assessment (which includes certification and testing procedures) for certain sectors as soon as possible. We will continue the ongoing work in several sectors and identify others for further work.
- We will endeavour to conclude by the end of 1996 a customs cooperation and mutual assistance agreement between the European Community and the US.
- To allow our people to take full advantage of newly developed information technology and services, we will work toward the realisation of a Transatlantic Information Society.
- Given the overarching importance of job creation, we pledge to cooperate in the follow-up to the Detroit Jobs Conference and to the G-7 Summit initiative. We look forward to further cooperation in the run up to the G-7 Jobs Conference in France, at the next G-7 Summit in the Summer of 1996 and in other fora such as the OECD. We will establish a joint working group on employment and labour-related issues.

IV   BUILDING BRIDGES ACROSS THE ATLANTIC

- We recognise the need to strengthen and broaden public support for our partnership. To that end, we will seek to deepen the commercial, social, cultural, scientific and educational ties among our people. We pledge to nurture in present and future generations the mutual understanding and sense of shared purpose that has been the hallmark of the post-war period.
- We will not be able to achieve these ambitious goals without the backing of our respective business communities. We will support and encourage the development of the transatlantic business relationship, as an integral part of our wider efforts to strengthen our bilateral dialogue. The successful conference of EU and US Business leaders which took place in Seville on 10-11 November 1995 was an important step in this direction. A number of its recommendations have already been incorporated into our Action Plan and we will consider concrete follow-up to others.
- We will actively work to reach a new comprehensive EC-US science and technology cooperation agreement by 1997.
- We believe that the recent EC-US Agreement on Cooperation in Education and Vocational Training can act as a catalyst for a broad spectrum of innovative cooperative activities of direct benefit to students and teachers. We will examine ways to increase private support for educational exchanges, including scholarship and internship programmes. We will work to introduce new technologies into classrooms, linking educational establishments in the EU with those in the US and will encourage teaching of each other's languages, history and culture.

Parliamentary links

We attach great importance to enhanced parliamentary links. We will consult parliamentary leaders on both sides of the Atlantic regarding consultative mechanisms, including those building on existing institutions, to discuss matters related to our transatlantic partnership.

Implementing our Agenda

The New Transatlantic Agenda is a comprehensive statement of the many areas for our common action and cooperation. We have entrusted the Senior Level Group to oversee work on this Agenda and particularly the priority actions we have identified. We will use our regular Summits to measure progress and to update and revise our priorities.

For the last fifty years, the transatlantic relationship has been central to the security and prosperity of our people. Our aspirations for the future must surpass our achievements in the past.

JOINT US-EU ACTION PLAN

This Action Plan for expanding and deepening EU-US relations reflects a framework with four shared goals:

* Promoting peace and stability, democracy and development around the world;
* Responding to global challenges;
* Contributing to the expansion of world trade and closer economic relations;
* Building bridges across the Atlantic.

I   PROMOTING PEACE AND STABILITY, DEMOCRACY AND DEVELOPMENT AROUND THE WORLD

We attach the highest importance to perfecting a new transatlantic community reflecting our joint interest in promoting stability and prosperity throughout the whole continent of Europe, based on the principles of democracy and free markets. We will cooperate both jointly and multilaterally to resolve tensions, support civil societies, and promote market reforms.

Our partnership is also global. We accept our responsibility to act jointly to resolve conflicts in troubled areas, to engage in preventive diplomacy together, to coordinate our assistance efforts, to deal with humanitarian needs and to help build in developing nations the capacity for economic growth and self-sufficiency. In this global partnership we are guided by the firm belief that the strengthening of democratic institutions and respect for human rights are essential to stability, prosperity and development.

1 Working together for a stable and prosperous Europe

a) Peace and reconstruction in the former Yugoslavia

We pledge to work boldly and rapidly, together and with other partners, to implement the peace, to assist recovery of the war-ravaged regions of the former Yugoslavia and to support economic and political reform and new democratic institutions.

We will cooperate to ensure: (1) respect for human rights, for the rights of minorities and for the rights of refugees and displaced persons, in particular the right of return; (2) respect for the work of the War Crimes Tribunal, established by the United Nations Security Council, in order to ensure international criminal accountability; (3) the establishment of a framework for free and fair elections in Bosnia-Herzegovina as soon as conditions permit and (4) the implementation of the agreed process for arms control, disarmament and confidence-building measures.

While continuing to provide humanitarian assistance, we will contribute to the task of reconstruction, subject to the implementation of the provisions of the peace settlement plan, in the context of the widest possible burden-sharing with other donors and taking advantage of the experience of international institutions, of the European Commission and of all relevant bilateral donors in the coordination mechanism.

We will continue to support the Bosnian-Croat Federation.

b) Central and Eastern European Countries

We will reinforce existing dialogue and cooperation on consolidating democracy, stability and the transition to market economies in Central and Eastern Europe. To this end, we will hold annual high-level consultations.

We will cooperate in support of the structural and micro-economic reforms in the countries of Central and Eastern Europe with a view to their integration into international political and economic institutions. We will continue to consult on ongoing technical assistance efforts to develop their financial systems and capital markets. We are fostering the creation of the legal and judicial infrastructure necessary in these countries to support expanded trade and investment.

We will pursue assistance cooperation on the spot in beneficiary countries via regular and intensified contacts between US missions and Commission Delegations, including assistance coordination meetings in selected capitals.

We will cooperate in helping the countries of Central and Eastern Europe to address their environmental problems by identifying joint projects consistent with the Lucerne Environmental Plan of Action, supporting the Budapest Regional Environmental Centre and building on proposals from the October 1995 Sofia Ministerial.

We will work together to promote economic reform in the countries participating in the Partners in Transition programme at the OECD, to facilitate their acceptance of OECD obligations and encourage their early accession. We will support the OECD's outreach efforts to the other Central and Eastern European countries seeking a closer relationship with the OECD.

c) Russia, Ukraine and other new independent states

We will reinforce existing dialogue and cooperation on consolidating democracy, stability and the transition to market economies in Russia, Ukraine and other new independent states (NIS). To this end, we will hold annual high-level consultations.

We will coordinate activities in support of the integration of Russia, Ukraine and other NIS in the global economy.

We will also reinforce the existing coordination relationship including technical assistance and enhanced on-the-spot coordination. We will:

- consider complementary initiatives such as: legal advice for reforms, tax reform, banking sector reform, human resources development, privatisation and post-privatisation activities, small and medium-sized enterprise development and democracy-building;

- intensify cooperation on projects aimed at protecting the environment in the fields endorsed by the Sofia Conference. In addition, we agree to take steps to establish an institution similar to the Budapest Regional Environmental Centre within the NIS.

We will continue to improve coordination on food assistance, using the successful coordination in the Caucasus as a practical example on which to build in future.

d) Turkey

We will support Turkish Government's efforts to strengthen democracy and advance economic reforms in order to promote Turkey's further integration into the transatlantic community.

e) Cyprus

We will work towards a resolution of the Cyprus question, taking into account the prospective accession of Cyprus to the European Union. We will support the UN Secretary General's Mission of Good Offices and encourage dialogue between and with the Cypriot communities.

2 Promoting the Middle East Peace Process

We will work together to make peace, stability and prosperity in the Middle East become a reality.
 To this end, we will:

- continue our support for Palestinian self-government and economic development;

- support the Palestinian elections which should contribute to the Palestinian democratic development;

- play an active role at the Conference for Economic Assistance to the Palestinians;

- work ambitiously to improve the access we both give to products from the West Bank and the Gaza Strip;

- encourage Jordanians, Palestinians, Israelis and Egyptians to establish comprehensive free trade arrangements among themselves;

- support the regional parties in their efforts to establish road links, electricity grids, gas pipelines and other joint infrastructure necessary to foster regional trade and investments;

- encourage and, as appropriate, support the regional parties in implementing the conclusions of the Amman Summit.

In addition, we will:

- continue our efforts to promote peace between Israel, Lebanon and Syria;

- actively seek the dismantling of the Arab boycott of Israel.

3 Sharing responsibility in other regions of the world

We will strengthen our joint efforts in preventive diplomacy, attacking the root causes of crisis and conflict, and will facilitate the movement from relief to long-term development.
We will:

- jointly assess the regional dimensions of the conflicts in Rwanda and in Burundi, jointly identify and plan for transitional priorities and support African-led regional initiatives to deal with these conflicts;

- support and participate in the UN/OAU sponsored Conference on the Great Lakes region;

- foster peace and economic reconstruction in Angola and Mozambique;

- take strong and appropriate steps to promote the rapid restoration of civilian democratic rules in Nigeria;

- intensify consultations in the field and deepen our policy dialogue, including on support for the consolidation and democratic institutions in El Salvador and Nicaragua;

- Support the peace process in Guatemala and the implementation of agreements among the parties;

- help Haiti to strengthen democracy and the rule of law by improving the effectiveness of its judicial system;

- promote democracy, economic reforms and human rights in Cuba;

- support smooth, successful transitions for Hong Kong and Macao in 1997 and 1999 respectively under the terms of the 1984 Sino-British and 1987 Sino-Portuguese Joint Declarations;

- work together to reduce the risk of regional conflict over the Korean peninsula, Taiwan and the South China Sea;

- reinforce our joint efforts to further the process of democratic reform in Burma;

- continue jointly to support the development of human rights and democratic practices in Cambodia; and

- continue to offer our strong support to the UN Secretary General in his efforts to find a lasting and just solution to the question of East Timor.

4 Development cooperation and humanitarian assistance

We have agreed to coordinate, cooperate and act jointly in development and humanitarian assistance activities.

To this end, we will establish a High-Level Consultative Group on Development Cooperation and Humanitarian Assistance to review progress of existing efforts, to assess policies and priorities and to identify projects and regions for the further strengthening of cooperation. This group will complement and reinforce existing coordination arrangements. The following areas for action have already been identified:

a) Development cooperation

We will:

- coordinate policies on democracy and civil society, on health and population, on development cooperation within the framework of international institutions and organisations on food security;

- develop a joint food security strategy in a number of selected countries;

- coordinate our support for sustainable development and economic reform in the context of political liberalisation in the Special Programme for Africa, cooperate in the Horn of Africa Initiative and on approaches vis-à-vis Southern Africa (including discussions with the Southern

Africa Development Community, the Common Market for Eastern and Southern Africa and the exploration of opportunities for collaborative long-term assessments);

- coordinate assistance policies to promote the participation of women at all levels.

b) *Humanitarian assistance*

We will:

- cooperate in improving the effectiveness of international humanitarian relief agencies, such as the United Nations High Commission for Refugees, the World Food Programme and the United Nations Department of Humanitarian Affairs, and in our planning and implementation of relief and reconstruction activities;

- consider joint missions whenever possible, starting in Northern Iraq, Liberia and Angola, and hold early consultations on security in refugee camps as well as on the use of military assets in humanitarian actions;

- work towards greater complementarity by extending operational coordination to include the planning phase, continuing and improving European Community-US operational information-sharing on humanitarian assistance, appointing EC-US humanitarian focal points on both sides of the Atlantic; and improving staff relations by exchange of staff and mutual training of officials administering humanitarian aid.

5 Human rights and democracy

We will:

- consult (bilaterally and within the framework of the relevant bodies of the UN, particularly the UN Commission on Human Rights) on countries where there is serious violation of human rights, in order to coordinate policies and, as appropriate, to develop joint initiatives;

- support jointly UN human rights activities, reinforcing the office of the UN High Commissioner on Human Rights and the Centre for Human Rights and following up UN conferences on human rights;

- ensure greater integration of the OSCE human dimension into conflict prevention and the daily activities of the OSCE (both regular meetings, contacts and missions on the ground);

- work to expand legal rights for women and to increase women's equal participation in decision-making processes, building on commitments made at the Fourth World Conference on Women in Beijing;

- aim at strengthening civics education in order to nurture the culture of democracy and, to that end, explore the possibility of EU participation in developing the coalition of public figures, educators, and private sector representatives established at the CIVITAS conference in Prague in June 1995.

6 Cooperation in international organisations

We will increase cooperation in developing a blueprint for UN economic and social reform including better coordination of UN activities, review of adjustment of agencies' mandates and adoption of more efficient management techniques with a more transparent and accountable Secretariat. We will cooperate to find urgently needed solutions to the financial crisis of the UN system. We are determined to keep our commitments, including our financial obligations. At the same time, the UN must direct its resources to the highest priorities and must reform in order to meet its fundamental goals.

We will cooperate to improve coherence in international economic organisations' activities, encouraging them to strengthen coordination between themselves and reduce overlap (e.g. between UN economic bodies, WTO, Bretton Words institutions, OECD).

We will strengthen coordination in the OSCE framework, including conflict prevention/crisis management, confidence- and security-building measures, and the economic dimension.

We will cooperate on global fisheries issues, in particular on the follow-up to the results of the UN Conference on Straddling Fish Stocks and Highly-Migratory Fish Stocks.

7 Non-proliferation, international disarmament and arms transfers

We will work together to promote Nuclear Non-Proliferation Treaty adherence by non-parties to the Treaty. We will coordinate actions to encourage non-adherents to act in accordance with the principle of non-proliferation.

We will combine our efforts to conclude in the Geneva Conference on Disarmament, in 1996, an effective, verifiable and universally applicable comprehensive Test Ban Treaty. We will undertake joint efforts for immediate negotiations on a Fissile Material Cut-Off Treaty.

We will coordinate on the prudent extension of the Missile Technology Control Regime to non-participating countries in order to control the spread of missile technology.

We will cooperate with a view to revising the 1972 Convention on Biological Weapons in order to promote new measures to increase its effectiveness. We will work to counter the proliferation of chemical and biological weapons.

We will support international efforts to curtail the use and proliferation of anti-personnel landmines (APLs). We will cooperate for a successful outcome of the Review Conference of the 1980 Convention on Prohibition and Restrictions on the Use of Certain Conventional Weapons, especially on the provisions relating to landmines. We will cooperate on the possible establishment of controls on the production, stockpiling and transfer of APLs.

We will continue efforts to establish anew multilateral arrangement for export controls - the New Forum - to respond to threats caused by the proliferation of arms and arms-related technologies as well as sensitive dual use items.

We will coordinate on preventing the spread of nuclear and other weapons of mass destruction, with particular emphasis on regions and countries of concern.

We will provide support to the Korean Peninsula Energy Development Organisation (KEDO), underscoring our shared desire to resolve important proliferation challenges throughout the world.

II   RESPONDING TO GLOBAL CHALLENGES

We share a common concern to address in an effective manner new global challenges which, without respect for national boundaries, present a serious treat to the quality of life and which neither of us can overcome alone. We pledge our actions and resources to meet together the challenges of international crime, terrorism and drug trafficking, mass migration, degradation of the environment, nuclear safety and disease. Together we can make a difference.

1 Fight against organised crime, terrorism and drug trafficking

We will cooperate in the fight against illegal drug trafficking, money laundering, terrorism, organised crime and illicit trade in nuclear materials.

We will enhance bilateral cooperation and institutional contacts. We will also enhance the capabilities of criminal justice and investigative systems and promote the rule of law through international training programmes at regional institutions such as the International Law Enforcement Academy in Budapest, the Italian Judicial Training Centre, the Middle and East European Police Academy and a similar administration of justice institution for the Western Hemisphere.

We will take steps to establish an information exchange mechanism on cooperation between the US and the EU and its member States in the law enforcement and criminal justice fields, especially regarding activities in providing training, technical assistance and equipment to other nations.

We will foster the exchange of law enforcement and criminal justice expertise between the US and the EU in three areas:

- scientific and technological developments;

- exchange of experts and observers between appropriate institutes and agencies;

- the sharing of information such as studies and analyses of emerging trends in international criminal activity.

When mutually agreed, we will jointly prepare reports to include recommended courses of action.

We will discuss the possibility of establishing interim cooperative measures between competent US authorities and the European Drugs Unit and begin implementing the possibilities for the convention on EUROPOL to facilitate relations between EUROPOL and the US Government.

We will examine possibilities for cooperation in support of the UN Drug Control Programme marine interdiction initiatives.

We will coordinate alternative development programmes to counter drug production.

We will jointly support the establishment of cooperative links between appropriate EU institutions such as the European Monitoring Centre for Drugs and Drug Addiction and the Comision Interamericana para el Control del Abuso de Drogas.

We will coordinate our counter-narcotics assistance programmes and projects in the Caribbean.

We will take action to strengthen the Dublin Group by reinforcing and supporting its members' counter-narcotic measures.

We will work to conclude an agreement in order to exchange, among other things, sensitive information for the pre-clearance of shipments of essential and precursor chemicals used in the production of illegal drugs and cooperate in joint training programmes in chemical diversion control.

We will cooperate on assessing and responding to terrorist threats.

2 Immigration and asylum

We will:

- strengthen information exchanges on illegal immigration and on asylum taking into account, inter alia, the work of the Geneva Intergovernmental Consultative Group;

- cooperate in the fight against the traffic in illegal immigrants;

- cooperate in the fight against the traffic in women;

- exchange information on asylum trends and on successful asylum system reform;

- establish common responses to refugee crisis situation, notably by early-warning mechanisms and coordination;

- develop a common stance on temporary protection in the United Nations High Commission for Refugees;

- coordinate positions on the Conference on Refugees and Migrants in the Commonwealth of Independent States;

- improve existing arrangements and exchanges of intelligence in areas of mutual concern, for example, forged identity documents and transport carriers' liability;

- convene seminars in 1996 and compare the results of our respective studies on migration flows both into the US and into the EU.

3 Legal and judicial cooperation

We will:

- identify means of strengthening international judicial assistance and cooperation in the obtaining of evidence and other relevant information;

- cooperate on the judicial seizure and forfeiture of assets;

- identify means to strengthen and improve international mechanisms for extradition, deportation, mutual legal assistance and other cooperative action to ensure that international fugitives have "nowhere to hide";

- cooperate in promoting the work of the Hague Conference on Private International Law and the International Institute for Unification of Private Law (UNIDROIT).

4 Preservation of the environment

We will enhance our exchange of views and coordination of negotiating positions on major global issues, with a view to improving the effectiveness of multilateral efforts to protect the global environment.

We will also strengthen the exchange of information and reporting on global environmental issues such as climate change, biodiversity, ozone layer depletion, persistent organic pollutants, desertification and erosion, water quality and quantity, land-based sources of marine pollution, hazardous wastes and contaminated soils, forest issues and trade and the environment.

We will work together at the UN Commission on Sustainable Development (CSD) and other relevant bodies, including the Global Environmental Facility, to encourage the world at large in the challenge of caring for the global environment. We will continue working on the successful conclusion of CSD work on the sustainable management of all types of forests.

We will enhance our bilateral dialogue on regulatory cooperation, including by:

- extending cooperation on chemicals issues, such as Prior Informed Consent for the trade in hazardous chemicals, harmonisation of classification and labelling, and reduction of risks from hazardous substances, building in particular on our joint call for actions in the OECD to reduce exposure to lead;

- continuing work on biotechnology issues such as the mutual acceptance of data to assessment and the release of genetically modified organisms;

- enhancing work on air pollution, including efforts to decrease emission from mobile sources and to assess the possibility of developing comparable emission standards.

We will undertake coordinated initiatives for the dissemination of environmental technologies, including in developing countries. In this regard, we will use the Climate Technology Initiative and proposals for an international clearinghouse on environmental technologies and practices. Private sector involvement will be a key aspect of this process.

We will engage in a broad and substantive dialogue on ways and means to limit and reduce global emission of greenhouse gases, including CO_2.

5 Population issues

We will coordinate to implement the International Conference on Population and Development ("Cairo Conference") Programme of Action. We will work to sustain support for family planning and expand access to reproductive health programmes in the context of a comprehensive approach to population stabilisation and sustainable development.

We will work together to strengthen the effectiveness of bilateral and multilateral population assistance programmes.

6 Nuclear safety

We will promote the ratification of the International Convention on Nuclear Safety.

We will coordinate positions in the negotiations in the International Convention on Radio-active Residues.

We will improve existing bilateral assistance coordination in the field of nuclear safety, extending to on-site and off-site nuclear emergency preparedness, including in the countries of Central and Eastern Europe and the NIS, as well as special G-7 Chernobyl assistance. We will cooperate in the preparation of the Moscow Conference on Nuclear Safety.

7 Health

We will establish an EU-US task force to develop and implement an effective global early warning system and response network for communicable diseases.

We are taking steps to provide for increased training opportunities and professional exchanges in the are of communicable diseases and encourage participation in EU and US programmes by scientists from developing countries.

We will coordinate our requests to other nations and to international organisations calling for action against emerging and re-emerging communicable diseases. We will encourage the follow-up of recent World Health Organisation (WHO) resolutions dealing with outbreak and reporting responsibilities and strengthened response centres.

We will cooperate, bilaterally and within the framework of the WHO, and other international organisations as appropriate, on respective programmes on health-related matters (AIDS and other communicable diseases, cancer, drug addiction) and identify specific areas for cooperation, especially in the research field.

III CONTRIBUTING TO THE EXPANSION OF WORLD TRADE AND CLOSER ECONOMIC RELATIONS

We are each other's largest trading and investment partners. Our economic prosperity is inextricably linked. At the same time, our economic and trade relations affect third countries and regions. It is our responsibility to contribute effectively to international economic stability and growth and to broaden our bilateral economic dialogue.

We have a special responsibility to strengthen the multilateral trading system, to support the World Trade Organisation and to lead the way in opening markets for trade and investment.

We will create a New Transatlantic Marketplace by progressively reducing or eliminating barriers that hinder the flow of goods, services and capital between us.

1 Strengthening the multilateral trading system

a) *Consolidating the WTO*

We will promote adherence to multilateral rules and commitments, including the effective functioning of the dispute settlement system, and secure the full implementation of the Uruguay Round Agreements by all WTO Members.

We will work to ensure a successful and substantive outcome for the Singapore Ministerial meeting.

We will cooperate on the accession of new members, notably China and Russia.

We will promote the effective management and operation of the WTO.

b) *Uruguay Round unfinished business*

We will work for the completion of the unfinished business of Marrakech with regard to goods and services. We are committed to the successful conclusion of the current negotiations in all services sectors by the agreed timetables. The most immediate deadlines are 30 April 1996 for telecommunications and 30 June 1996 for maritime services.

c) *Financial services*

We agree to concert our efforts to promote liberalisation of financial service son a worldwide basis. In particular, we will seek to ensure that the interim agreement concluded in July 1995 is succeeded by a more substantial package of permanent liberalisation commitments from a critical mass of WTO members.

d) *Government procurement*

We will promote the launching by Ministers in Singapore of negotiations within the WTO aimed at covering substantially all government procurement and WTO members.

e)   Intellectual property rights (IPR)

We will cooperate to ensure the full implementation of the TRIPs
Agreement and improve the level of IPR protection throughout the world.
We will work to develop a comprehensive agenda for future TRIPs
negotiations within the WTO.

f)   New issues

We will work together in the WTO and/or other appropriate fora. We will
give priority to:
    Environment: The report to the Singapore Ministerial Meeting should
set out clear recommendations for decisions and a process for further work
to ensure that trade and environmental measures are mutually supportive.

(i)   Investment: We will work closely together in formulating our
       respective policies. This cooperation should, in particular, bear
       fruit in a successful conclusion, as called for in the 1995 OECD
       Ministerial Declaration, of the negotiations on a Multilateral
       Agreement on Investment (MAI) espousing strong principles on
       international investment liberalisation and protection. Meanwhile,
       we will work to develop discussion of the issue with our partners
       in the WTO.

(ii)   Competition: We will pursue work on the scope for multilateral
       action in the fields of trade and competition policy.   Our
       competition authorities will cooperate in working with other
       countries to develop effective antitrust regimes.

(iii) Labour standards: We will join our efforts in the WTO and other
       fora with a view to dissipating various misunderstandings and
       preoccupations of trading partners regarding the relationship
       between trade and internationally recognised labour standards.

g)   Market access: creating additional trading opportunities

We will cooperate in creating additional trading opportunities, bilaterally
and throughout the world, in conformity with our WTO commitments. In
view of the importance of the information society, we are launching a
specific exercise in order to attempt to conclude an information technology
agreement.

In the perspective of the WTO Singapore Ministerial Meeting, we will explore the possibility of agreeing on a mutually satisfactory package of tariff reductions on industrial products, and we will consider which, if any, Uruguay Round obligations on tariffs can be implemented on a accelerated basis.

We will work ambitiously to improve the access we both give to products from the West Bank and Gaza Strip.

h) International customs cooperation

We will work together in the World Customs Organisation and cooperate with the International Chamber of Commerce to develop a comprehensive model of norms and standards for customs procedures throughout the work to promote inter alia increased transparency and harmonised approaches to classification, valuation and rules of origin.

i) Illicit payments

We will combat corruption and bribery by implementing the 1994 OECD Recommendation on Bribery in International Transactions.

2 The New Transatlantic Marketplace

The creation of the New Transatlantic Marketplace will include the following actions, which also take into consideration the recommendations of the Transatlantic Business Dialogue:

a) Joint study

We will carry out a joint study on ways of facilitating trade in goods and services and further reducing or eliminating tariff and non-tariff barriers.

b) Confidence building

As part of a confidence-building process, we will reinforce our efforts to resolve bilateral trade issues and disputes.

c) *Standards, certification and regulatory issues*

We will claim to conclude an agreement on mutual recognition of conformity assessment (which includes certification and testing procedures) for certain sectors as soon as possible. We will continue the ongoing work in several sectors and identify others for further work.

We will cooperate closely in the international standard setting process, drawing on international bodies to achieve the greatest possible use of international standards, and will seek the maximum practical transparency, participation and non-discrimination.

We will devote special attention to cooperatively developing and implementing regulations on vehicle safety requirements and on measures to reduce air and noise emission. We will build on existing efforts aimed at facilitating international harmonisation, taking account of our respective policies on safety and environmental protection, while recognising the need to achieve, wherever possible, global regulatory uniformity.

We will strengthen regulatory cooperation, in particular by encouraging regulatory agencies to give a high priority to cooperation with their respective transatlantic counterparts, so as to address technical and other non-tariff barriers to trade resulting from divergent regulatory processes. We will especially encourage a collaborative approach between the EU and the US in testing and certification procedures by promoting greater compatibility of standards and health- and safety related measures. To this end, we will seek to develop pilot cooperative projects.

d) *Veterinary and plant health issues*

We will conclude an agreement to establish a framework for determining equivalence of veterinary standards and procedures for all live animals and animal products.

We will enhance the established cooperation on plant health issues and in the area of pesticide residues regulation.

e) *Government procurement*

We will aim to increase substantially in 1996 and beyond the coverage of EU/US bilateral commitments on public procurement under the Government Procurement Agreement and to coordinate in developing proposals on information technology under the Agreement.

f)   *Intellectual property rights (IPR)*

With a view to reinvigorating our efforts to solve remaining IPR problems, we will hold a seminar during 1996 addressing current and future IPR issues.

g)   *Financial services*

We will expand our ongoing dialogue on financial services to include discussion of the financial and economic aspects of our respective relations with third countries.

h)   *Customs cooperation*

We will endeavour to conclude by the end of 1996 a customs cooperation and mutual assistance agreement between the EC and the US. The agreement should cover:

- customs cooperation: simplification of customs procedures, computer-isation (information, data exchange, common access to databases etc.), consultation within international organisations, methods of work;

- mutual assistance: exchange of enforcement information, increased investigative cooperation in customs matters, protection of intellectual property rights, commercial fraud, illicit nuclear traffic, trade in severely restricted chemicals;

- programmes for the exchange of officials.

i)   *Information Society, information technology and telecom-munications*

We will expand and develop the bilateral Information Society Dialogue, in order to further common understanding of global issues implying access to information services through public institutions, regulatory reforms, and technological cooperation, including the continuation of expert-level discussions in the following areas:

- interconnection and interoperability, including standardisation issues (particularly for interfaces, network equipment, mobile telephones, digital video broadcasting/high definition television);

- universal service;

- procompetitive interconnection policies and principles;

- access to information and the protection of IPR;

- satellite policy;

- commercial communications;

- privacy and data protection;

- the impact on society, including public services and employment.

The Dialogue will also address those new legislative and regulatory developments which are proposed or are being prepared to achieve progress in these areas, including questions of regulatory transparency.

In the context of enhance cooperation in science and technology, we will work towards the reduction of obstacles to cooperation in research and development in the field of information and communication. We will jointly support the implementation of the G-7 global projects on the Information Society, aiming to spur innovation and ensure interconnection and interoperability. Furthermore, we will exchange information on on-ongoing and future research programmes in the field of information communication technology to foster concrete bilateral cooperation actions in research and development.

We will also discuss regulatory issues relating to online interactive and international service provision, in order to maximise their development, which is essential for the success of the transition towards an Information Society on both sides of the Atlantic.

We will cooperate on the integration of developing countries into the global Information Society, initially through our support for the Information Society Conference in South Africa in 1996 and through our participation in the International Telecommunications Union.

j) Competition

We will pursue, and build on, bilateral cooperation in the immediate term based on the EC-US Agreement of 1991. We will examine the options for deepening cooperation on competition matters, including the possibility of a further agreement.

k) Data protection

We will discuss data protection issues with a view to facilitating information flows, while addressing the risks to privacy.

l) Transport

We will:

- establish a working group for consultations on design and implementation of Global Navigation Satellite Systems;

- improve EU-US cooperation on air traffic management;

- hold consultations on maritime transport safety and crew qualifications.

m) Energy

We will intensify contacts and cooperation on energy-related issues - including through contacts in multilateral fora where appropriate - such as the environmental implications of energy policy on regulatory frameworks for the energy sector, on technical assistance activities to third countries and on energy technology.

n) Biotechnology

We will encourage regulatory cooperation, including with respect to genetically modified organisms, and expanded bilateral cooperation in the preparation of multilateral meetings and negotiations in connection with the UN, FAO, OECD, CODEX Alimentarius and the Biodiversity Convention.

We will continue the activities of the EU-US Biotechnology Task Force, and in this context, will promote joint research efforts in the fields of neuro-informatics and marine biotechnology.

o)   Safety and health

We will explore the scope for an agreement for the exchange of information on issues affecting health and safety at work, such as occupational safety and health standards, the development of regulations, high risk activity, carcinogenic substances at the workplace, toxicology, testing education and information programmes, and the collection of statistics and data.

We will explore the establishment of improved mechanisms for the timely exchange of information related to the general safety of products, including the withdrawals of products from the market.

3 Jobs and growth

Given the overarching importance of job creation, we pledge to cooperate in the follow-up to the Detroit Jobs Conference and the G-7 Summit initiative. We look forward to further cooperation in the run-up to the G-7 Jobs Conference in France, at the next G-7 Summit in the Summer of 1996 and in other fora such as the OECD and the International Labour Organisation.

We will establish a joint working group on employment and labour-related issues. We will intensify the dialogue, in particular on new forms of labour-management cooperation; increased investment in human resources, including in education and skills training; smoothing the transition from school-to-work and job-to-job; active labour market policies and the relationship between work and welfare; employment and new technologies; and encouraging entrepreneuralism.

We will continue to exchange view on macroeconomic issues in the light of the importance of a sound macroeconomic framework both for the development of an harmonious relationship and for the fostering of non-inflationary growth, the reduction of imbalances and international financial stability.

IV   BUILDING BRIDGES ACROSS THE ATLANTIC

We recognise that the transatlantic relationship can be truly secure in the coming century only if future generations understand its importance as well as their parents and grandparents did. We are committed to fostering an active and vibrant transatlantic community by deepening and broadening the commercial, social, cultural, scientific and educational ties that bind us.

1 Transatlantic Business Dialogue

We will support and encourage the development of the Transatlantic Business Dialogue, as an integral part of our wider efforts to strengthen our bilateral relationship. The successful conference of EU and US business leaders which took place in Seville on 10-11 November 1995 was an important step in this direction. We welcome the fact that the participants were able to agree on a series of joint recommendations to build an even stronger framework within which trade, investment, capital and technology can flow across the Atlantic. We commend them for encouraging both business communities to continue to devote attention to possible improvements in the transatlantic commercial relationship.

We have studied carefully the recommendations adopted at Seville, and have already incorporated a number of them into our present Action Plan. Our officials will work closely together with our business leaders on both sides in considering follow-up to the many other suggestions arising from the Seville meeting, and will report at the next EU-US Summit.

2 Broadening science and technology cooperation

We will negotiate a new, comprehensive EC-US science and technology cooperation agreement by 1997 based on the principle of mutual interest, with a view to achieving a balance of benefits to us both.

We will work to conclude the Agreement on Intelligent Manufacturing Systems (advanced technologies and robotics).

Recognising that scientific and technological advances underlie our ability to meet global challenges and foster economic growth, we will promote cooperative science and technology projects in support of topics identified in this document.

In addition, we will work to identify collaborative projects and exchange information to address cross-border issues such as transportation, health and global climate change. Examples of specific projects include: intermodal transport and fast transhipment techniques; intelligent transportation systems; the study and forecasting of travel behaviour; development of a malaria vaccine; and the study of environmental health and the effects of radiation.

3 People to people links

We will:

- encourage our citizens to increase their contacts in diverse fora - youth, professionals, think tanks, etc. - with a view to deepening grass roots support for the transatlantic relationship and enriching the flow of ideas for the solution of common problems;

- work for the early creation of the joint consortia and for the implementation of the Fulbright Awards and other activities provided for in our Agreement on Cooperation in Higher Education and Vocational Training;

- cooperate on the reform of higher education in the countries of Central and Eastern Europe, Russia, Ukraine, other NIS and Mongolia by identifying and assessing those projects of the EU's TEMPUS programme which already include US partner universities and exploring possibilities of wider participation of US universities in TEMPUS projects;

- encourage the study of each other's systems of government as well as the histories, cultures and languages of our communities;

- encourage voluntary cooperation and dissemination of information for the mutual recognition of university studies and degrees within the EU Member States and the US;

- examine ways to increase private support for educational exchanges, including scholarships and intern programmes;

- exchange information and cooperate on innovations related to vocational training and intend to convene a conference on vocational training in Spring 1996;

- examine ways new technologies might be employed to link education and training establishments, including schools in the EU with those in the US;

- encourage "sister cities" to promote exchanges.

4 Information and Culture

We will study ways and means of:

- encouraging artistic and cultural cooperation projects, such as exchanges in the field of the visual arts, theatre, ballet, orchestras and musical groups, the co-production of films and TV programmes;

- spreading knowledge of and encouraging literary creativity, including exploring with the private sector the sponsorship of an EU-US prize for literature;

- spreading knowledge of cultural and artistic heritage programmes.

We will use our sites on the INTERNET to provide quick and easy access to the New Transatlantic Agenda, the Joint EU-US Action plan, information on EU and US studies, descriptions of pertinent library holdings as well as other material relevant to the EU-US relationship.

We will consult and cooperate on the preparation of a medium-term communications strategy which will aim to increase public awareness on both sides of the Atlantic of the EU-US dimension.

Appendix II
Transatlantic Business Dialogue - Overall Conclusions From the 11 November 1995 Seville Conference

General remarks

The European and US business leaders meeting at Sevilla express their thanks to the US and EU political authorities for taking the initiative in calling this conference and for giving the business community an opportunity to contribute to the development of the Trans-Atlantic marketplace. They also express their warm appreciation for the hospitality provided by the Spanish Government as hosts for the conference.

The business community gives this central message to their political leaders: that the Trans-Atlantic business relationship is one of the great successes of the post-war world. It produces massive advantages not only for the companies directly involved but for millions of employees and customers. It is also one of the driving forces for the entire world economic system. The business community urges our governments to eliminate, as soon as possible, the remaining obstacles to trade and investment.

The bilateral EU-US relationship must be seen in the context of world-wide multilateral cooperation based on overall macroeconomic and monetary coordination. This includes full support for the rules and principles of the World Trade Organisation (WTO) and other relevant institutions, and the need to ensure any bilateral or plurilateral agreements are WTO compatible.

Business leaders also emphasise that this business initiative is only one element in a larger dialogue, and that the Trans-Atlantic marketplace can only flourish against the background of a vigorous and whole-hearted political cooperation based on mutual respect and trust.

Sevilla was a successful meeting, because the priorities were developed by the chief executives of companies which are already deeply engaged in business on both sides of the Atlantic. They came to Sevilla, not to negotiate between US and EU industry but to present joint recommendations which they believe are widely supported by their colleagues in other companies and industries, many of whom were involved in the preparatory work. The recommendations reflect the broad thrust of agreement among participants, even though some participants might not necessarily support the specific elements of each recommendation.

Principal objectives

Our common goal is to keep both Europe and the US competitive in the world economy. Our ability to meet this global challenge requires common efforts to create the right framework conditions for trade, investment, research and development.

Competitiveness is hampered both by excessive regulation and by differences between EU and US regulatory systems. Political leaders should analyse the competitive situation of industry on both sides of the Atlantic and ensure that laws and regulations converge wherever necessary to allow market forces to accelerate economic growth and job creation and to improve international competitiveness.

Business therefore calls on the political leaders to make every effort:

- to support and develop the Trans-Atlantic business relationship, and the growth of the Trans-Atlantic marketplace;

- to build a strong framework within which trade, investment, capital and technology flow freely across the Atlantic;

- to remove all obstacles and public policy impediments so that business can operate on either side of the ocean without any unfair constraint or discrimination;

- to help other countries acquire full and open access to the world-wide free market trading system and its benefits, rules and disciplines within the principles of Most Favoured National (MFN); and

- to help to develop a secure framework for international investment.

Against this background the participants in the Trans-Atlantic Business Dialogue urge political leaders to give the most careful consideration to the specific recommendations of the four working groups operating in the Sevilla Conference. The recommendations are attached in Annex to this statement.

Follow-up Procedures

Business executives, companies and organisations are ready to support each of these recommendations with detailed proposals and analysis. What matters now is to follow up this work and achieve specific action and concrete results. The responsibility for doing so rests with government and business.

The Sevilla Conference therefore calls on the EU and US governments to study these documents with great care and to incorporate their message into the statement from the EU-US summit meeting in Madrid, Spain, on 3 December.

The Steering Committee which prepared the Sevilla Conference will meet again in January and seek a report on government action. Based on the governments' response, the business community will then make specific proposals on the next stages of our work.

As an initial step, the co-chairmen of the conference have agreed that Alex Trotman and Jürgen Strube will identify the best means of using existing resources and organisations to press for implementation of these recommendations, to refine the specific action required, and to continue the dialogue on issues needing further study. A follow-up meeting will be arranged in the US in 1996.

The US and European business leaders meeting at Sevilla are determined to take this process further. Action is needed to liberalise trade and investment, to remove public policy impediments to the operation of the market and to encourage cooperation on wider international issues. Such action will do more than almost anything else to build prosperity and create jobs.

Conference Co-Chairmen:
Paul Allaire, Xerox
Jürgen Strube, BASF
Peter Sutherland, Goldman Sachs International
Alex Trotman, Ford

In Annex: *Full recommendations from the four working groups.*

Working group I -- Standards, certification and regulatory policy
Final recommendations

I.1   Mutual recognition

Full and complete Mutual Recognition Agreement (MRAs) negotiations for medical devices, telecommunications terminal equipment, information technology products, and electrical equipment and a common transatlantic registration dossier for new drug products should be completed by no later than January 1, 1997. Talks on MRAs in additional product sectors should be initiated based on the recommendations of the transatlantic advisory committee. These new MRAs should build upon and expand on the current talks that should conclude as soon as possible. Before an MRA covering medical devices can be concluded, the US must enact meaningful regulatory reform legislation.

I.2   Common standards

The EU and US should aim to develop and adopt common and open standards wherever possible based on international product standards such as those of the ISO and IEC, where appropriate and supported by industry. In the development of common and open standards in areas of rapidly advancing technology the aim should be the adoption of widely accepted de facto standards led by industry. A good example of the need for harmonisation is the motor vehicle sector. The EU and US must commit themselves to harmonising vehicle regulations beginning with safety requirements and environmental emissions. Future divergence should be prevented by joining together in a global regulatory forum such as the UN-ECE Working Party 29. Mutual recognition for testing and certification should be achieved. By April 1996 (and at regular six-month intervals thereafter), relevant EU and US regulators, including the US National Highway Traffic Safety Administration (NHTSA) and the European Commission, should report on progress made toward achieving these objectives. Another example of the need to move toward common approaches is international protection of copyright and security for rightholders, particularly over the global information infrastructure. To provide the development of this infrastructure and enable universal access, there must be common and open functional standards in areas such as encryption, data protection and interoperability. The ultimate aim of any reform efforts should be the adoption of harmonised standards, certification and regulatory policies around the world that will enable products to be approved once and accepted everywhere.

I.3   Regulatory cooperation

There should be increased transparency and cooperation between the EU and US in standards-setting, compliance requirements, product approvals and certification procedures, though regulatory agency or government programs should be avoided where there is no overriding concern for oversight or control. The US industry-led, private sector standard setting bodies should engage in timely and effective cooperation with their EU counterparts towards achieving greater harmonisation in the area of minimum requirements and in the meantime, work towards mutual recognition. Specific sectors will be recommended for consideration by the transatlantic advisory committee.

I.4   Transparency, participation, and non-discrimination

The principles of transparency, participation, timeliness and non-discrimination must be adhered to in any standards-setting process. Standards development organisations and the procedures that drive these bodies must be open to all participants in the EU and US. The European Committee for Standardisation (CEN), the European Committee for Electrotechnical Standardisation (CENELEC) and the European Telecommunications Standards Institute (ETSI) should extend membership on the basis of reciprocity to non-EU standards-setting bodies, as US standards-setting bodies currently do with all foreign participants.

I.5   Use of functional-based standards

Technical regulations set by government should rely on functional standards. Design specifications, research and development and manufacturing processes and product-specific standards should be avoided. The transatlantic advisory committee will identify product sectors in which design specifications are used and recommend steps for their immediate elimination.

I.6   Manufacturer's declaration of conformity

Efforts to streamline testing and certification rules must be based primarily on the manufacturer's declaration of conformity. By March 1996, the transatlantic advisory committee will identify sectors where greater use of manufacturer's declaration of conformity is required, and make recommendations to regulatory authorities accordingly.

I.7   Obstacles to free circulation

The EU and US should ensure that existing and proposed functional requirements do not discriminate against products which are not locally produced. Policy instruments which may in some instances operate as disguised "local preference vehicles", including some environmental regulations, should be avoided. Environmental standards should be based on scientifically proven criteria. Obstacles to free circulation in the form of different functional requirements should be identified by the transatlantic advisory committee and progressively eliminated with the aim of permitting products to circulate freely within and between the EU and the US.

I.8   Consistency with multilateral liberalisation

Future talks between the US and US on standards and regulatory reform must be based on the principles of open trade as reflected in the multilateral rule sand disciplines of the WTO Technical Barriers to Trade (TBT) Agreement. By January 1, 1996, the EU and US should develop a set of reform proposals for discussion at the WTO, taking into consideration the recommendations from the transatlantic advisory committee.

I.9   Telecommunications

The EU and US must quickly reach an appropriate agreement on an accelerated basis in the pending WTO negotiations on telecommunications. EU and US firms should have the freedom to offer basic telecommunication services under commercially viable terms and conditions. There should be no restrictions on EU or US firm's foreign investment or ownership including liberalisation in the area of national media regulations.

I.10   Political commitment to reforming standards, certification and regulatory policy

At the Madrid US/EU Summit in December 1995, President Clinton, Commission President Santer and European Council President Gonzalez should issue a statement which makes a long terms political commitment to concrete reform of standards, certification and regulatory policy aimed at reducing or eliminating the impact of these policies as barriers to trade and commerce.

I.11   Transatlantic advisory committee

At the Madrid EU-US Summit in December 1995, government leaders should announce the creation of a Transatlantic Advisory Committee on Standards, Certification and Regulatory Policy made up to EU and US representatives of government bodies and industry to provide guidance and to monitor progress in achieving reform in these areas.   The TABD EU-US Advisory Committee should be established by January 1996.   The committee should present its first action plan identifying priority areas, a timetable for progress and practical steps to achieve the stated goals.

Working group II -- Trade liberalisation
Final recommendations

Multilateral system

The joint commitment of the EU and the US to uphold the multilateral process and to establish the WTO on a solid basis is crucial to the future of an open world trading system and healthy economic bilateral relationships.

II.1   Both parties should work together to conclude current WTO initiatives within the timetable and to build the WTO into a strong, objective and decisive body.

II.2   The EU and the US should maintain the momentum of the multilateral process by working together on a new agenda for the world trade liberalisation.   The first priority is to complete the unfinished business of the Uruguay Round.

II.3   The US and the EU should fully implement the UR agreements, including the agreement on TRIPS, TRIMS and GATS.

II.4   The EU and US governments should commit resources to develop joint recommendations for the future world programme of the WTO. A transparent process should be established for the business community to provide input on matters of mutual interest (such as harmonisation of non-preferential rules of origin).

II.5 Both governments should ensure that all new regional arrangements by the EU and the US are WTO compatible, thereby effectively strengthening the multilateral trading system.

Tariffs

II.6 At the request of specific sectors establish transatlantic working groups to consider which, if any, UR obligations on tariffs or other matters can be implemented on an accelerated basis and to consider as well additional cuts or elimination of duties in sectors not now due to go to zero. Both sides cited European industry proposals for tariff for chemicals as models for bilateral industry collaboration leading to trade liberalisation.

II.7 The US and EU should come to rapid agreement, by the end of 1995, on compensation owed for tariff increases resulting from the accession of Austria, Finland and Sweden.

Information Technology Agreement (ITA)

II.8 As provided in the ITA, both governments should make a commitment to conclude negotiations of the ITA by December 1996. Conclude an Information Technology Agreement between the EU and US. It is the view of the overwhelming majority that the ITA package should include a commitment to eliminate all tariffs by 1 January 2000 or sooner.

II.9 The EU and US industries agree that they must cooperate on the development of a Global Information Infrastructure (GII) to remove as quickly as possible the market access barriers for Information Technology.

Trade and competition policy

II.10 The EU and US should use existing comity procedures in antitrust enforcement.

II.11 EU-US efforts to increase the exchange of information must proceed in consultation with business.

II.12 The EU and US should develop convergent procedures to vet mergers.

II.13 The US and the EU should agree to make world-wide "market access" for all companies, foreign and domestic, a priority objective. The EU and the US should seek harmonisation of strong and effective competition policies within WTO.

II.14 The US and EU should actively support the OECD's efforts to establish multilateral guidelines for the development of competition policies that allow unimpaired market access for foreign goods, services, ideas, investments and business people, so that they are able to benefit from the opportunity to compete in a market on terms equal or comparable to those enjoyed by local competitors.

Customs administration

II.15 The US and the EU should make convergence and modernisation of customs practices, including improvements in information sharing and automation, a matter of high priority.

Specific steps to be discussed:
- establishment of a consultative process for foreign customs authorities within the framework of Customs 2000;
- collaborative efforts to identify and follow "best customs practices";
- harmonisation of required entry data, formats and retention periods.

II.16 The US and the EU should support the development and promotion of a model for an efficient and uniform customs administration, including for example, the initiatives of the World Customs Organisation (WCO) and the International Chamber of Commerce (ICC).

II.17 Encourage EU and US governments to conclude WCO/WTO efforts to harmonise non-preferential rules of origin within agreed upon time frames.

II.18 The US and the EU should improve the administration of current customs procedures in order to reduce the cost of Trans-Atlantic transactions, including examination of upward reclassification problems associated with changing technologies.

II.19 The appropriate US and EU authorities should report to the mid-year 1996 US-EU Presidential meeting and to appropriate US-European business organisations on the most rapid timetable feasible for implementing a comprehensive model.

II.20 The US and EU authorities should conclude a bilateral Customs Cooperation and Mutual Assistance Agreement.

Product liability

II.21 The US and European business community supports the efforts to develop national product liability legislation in the US that should adopt principles of predictability, consistency and fairness.

Transportation

II.22 The US and the EU should lead the way in negotiating multilateral agreements on transportation services that provide for open access and operating flexibility both on a Trans-Atlantic basis and within the US and the EU with the aim of reducing transaction costs.

Government procurement

II.23 Governments should agree to implement fully existing commitments and obligations under the Government Procurement Code.

II.24 In order to sustain open and equitable access for EU/US companies to the respective public procurement markets, the public procurement legislation should be expeditiously implemented and restrictions should be in line with art. 8 GPC.

II.25 The US and European business community will identify existing national preferences in government procurement and develop recommendations for their elimination, where appropriate.

Common eligibility for R&D programmes

II.26 The Transatlantic Business Dialogue should advocate conclusion of common eligibility standards to govern access to research and development programmes. National treatment should be the cornerstone of an agreement reached between the EU and US that is applicable in the US and the Members States of the European Union. Transatlantic business should urge governments to reach agreement by December 1996.

Intellectual property rights

II.27 The EU and the US should promote the effective protection world-wide of intellectual property rights by implementing and extending TRIPS and building on other initiatives including the G7 Business Roundtable Recommendations.

II.28 The US should enter into discussions to determine whether the objective of introducing a first-to-file system in the United States would be appropriate in the context of a balanced package of improvements in patent systems outside the United States.

II.29 The EU should reduce the costs associated with securing patent protection by reducing duplication of effort by sharing the tasks of patent search and examination between the US Patent and Trademark Office and the European Patent Office.

II.30 The US and the EU should work closely together in bilateral, plurilateral, and multilateral fora such as WIPO to ensure that the content transmitted over the Global Information Infrastructure is adequately protected.

Trade and environment

II.31 The US and the EU should work to establish common approaches to environmental issues through appropriate fora.

II.32 The US and EU should not use unilateral trade measures (e.g. measures based on processes and production methods) as a means to impose their own environmental standards for risk management preferences on each other.

Monetary stability

II.33 Better monetary stability should be fostered.

Continuing trade liberalisation

II.34 EU/US members of the working group II agreed that, after having studied a list of 11 different items related to trade liberalisation, EU and US governments, with the support of industrial experts, should take all possible measures to liberalise as much as possible, and in a step-by-step approach and in conformity with WTO provisions, the trade between US and EU.

This pragmatic approach should take into account following priorities:
- full implementation of the Uruguay Round and the unfinished businesses within WTO;
- establishment at the request of specific sectors of Trans-Atlantic working groups to consider acceleration of Uruguay Round tariffs and other obligations, as well as additional tariff cuts;
- gradual harmonisation of strong and effective trade and competition policies within WTO;
- convergence and modernisation of customs practices including conclusion of a Customs Cooperation and Mutual Assistance Agreement; and
- full implementation of government procurement commitment and obligations.

II.35 The US and the EU should through the existing channels undertake a joint study of issues in trade liberalisation, which should be distinguished from existing "trade barrier" reports in that it would identify targets for continuing liberalisation. The US and European business community will produce an annual list of priority trade liberalisation needs.

Business experts in specific existing organisations on both sides of the Atlantic should start consultations on the bilateral issues. They should be assisted by governmental representatives.

Working group III - Investment
Final recommendations

A.   Open investment regimes and national treatment

EU and US businesses have been able to succeed and to provide the engine of growth for the Atlantic area. Governments on both sides of the Atlantic have supported an open, stable environment for investment. Policies that have worked so well to our mutual advantage deserve to be recognised, enhanced, and commended to others as crucial to achieve economic and social progress.

Recognising that foreign investment is critical for firms to compete in today's global economy and that benefits of foreign owned investment accrue to home and host countries alike, the TABD conferees urge the following:

III.1 The US, the EU and/or its Member States should issue a comprehensive statement at the Madrid Summit that expresses their shared commitment to open investment regimes. This statement should reaffirm the commitment of the United States and the European Union to the principle of national treatment for investors and investments.

III.2 The US, the EU and/or the Member States should work towards the goal of a multilateral agreement on investment that embodies the highest standards for liberalisation and investment protection. This agreement should be concluded as soon as possible on a multilateral basis covering the widest number of countries.

III.3 A multilateral agreement on investment should include:

a) a broad definition of investment;

b) the highest standards of investment protection;

c) the better of national treatment (NT) or Most Favoured Nation (MFN) treatment;

d) provisions for non-discrimination among signatory countries to the agreement and strong Most Favoured Nation (MFN) disciplines;

e) provisions for further liberalisation of the investment regimes, both upon entry into force of the agreement and afterwards;

f) full transparency of the rules and of the remaining restrictions;

g) an effective dispute settlement mechanism that will afford investors recourse against government actions; and

h) provisions that bind sub-federal authorities.

B.   Issues not related to the multilateral agreement on investment

III.4   Taxation. The US, the EU and/or its Member States should reaffirm their intention to abide by the new OECD Transfer Pricing Guidelines, including at the sub-federal level, and to support private sector (BIAC) participation in a future OECD monitoring mechanism;

III.5   The US, the EU and/or its Member States should restate their rejection of formulary apportionment;

III.6   The US, the EU and/or its Member States should reject pressure from national legislatures to pursue discriminatory tax legislation, policies and practices which discriminate against foreign companies.

III.7   The US, the EU and/or its Member States should review and modify their respective tax laws on the treatment of foreign earned income to encourage Trans-Atlantic investment.

III.8   Monetary Stability. Recognising that monetary stability is important to a good investment climate, the business community stresses the importance of improving the economic fundamentals that underlie monetary stability.

III.9   R&D Access. The US, the EU and/or its Member States should work to improve access to each others' government funded, civilian research and development programs.

III.10 Extortion and bribery. The US, the EU and/or its Member States should fully implement the 1994 OECD Recommendations on bribery in international transactions. Follow up to the OECD recommendations should include review and change of relevant tax legislation, regulations and practices.

III.11 Movement of people. The US, the EU and/or its Member States should review their existing immigration and/or labour law requirements and work together to eliminate barriers to free movement of personnel and their immediate families for business purposes.

III.12 Public Procurement. The US, the EU and/or its Member States should fully implement existing commitments and obligations under the WTO Code on Government Procurement. At an appropriate time, they should renew their efforts to eliminate the remaining procurement restrictions at the central and sub-central levels. In addition, they should work together to encourage non-signatory countries to subscribe to the agreement.

III.13 National Security. National security exceptions should be limited, narrowly prescribed, and implemented in a manner consistent with the intent and spirit of an open investment regime.

III.14 Reports To Business. Six months after the Seville Conference, officials of the European Union and the United States should report on the responses of their governments to the recommendations provided to them by the participants in the Trans-Atlantic Business Dialogue on November 11, 1995.

III.15 The business Communities of the United States and Europe should monitor the progress made with respect to these US and European recommendations on investment through appropriate, existing business channels.

Working group IV -- Third country issues
Final recommendations

IV.1 Introduction
The United States and the EU should, in future trade discussions, make use of the unique and important consultative opportunity provided by the TABD to take into account the views of the private sector on trade and commercial policy issues.

IV.2 Government Procurement
Serious efforts should be made by the EU and the United States in order to expand the adoption of the WTO Agreement on Public Procurement to countries whose public procurement practices remain closed. Specific emphasis should be placed upon transparency, effective implementation and enforcement in their domestic legislation and regulations of all the Agreement's provisions.

IV.3 International Customs Standards
The World Customs Organisation and the International Chamber of Commerce are currently working to develop international customs models that will set norms and standards for customs procedures. The

United States and the EU, together with United States and EU business communities and interested trade associations, should support these efforts. The United States and EU business community can also play an important role by bringing customs abuses to the attention of the appropriate government agencies.

IV.3a The United States and the EU should consider identifying those elements to receive priority and working in concert to promote adoption of those elements. Important elements that could be adopted in the near term include greater transparency, the Harmonised Tariff System, and the WTO Valuation Agreement. For example, pre-shipment inspection procedures should not be used to jeopardise and restrict trade. APEC negotiations have created an opportunity to promote the elements of the ICC model.

IV.4a Intellectual Property Rights
The United States and the EU should together push for complete implementation and enforcement by other countries of the Uruguay Round agreement on Trade-Related Aspects of Intellectual Property Rights (TRIPs) and for its extension to countries that are not currently signatories to the accord.

IV.4b The United States and the EU should seek to ensure the closing of the gaps in the coverage of the TRIPs agreement (such as the permissible exceptions from patent coverage for plant and animal varieties and the escape clause for protecting confidential information) as TRIPs is extended to other countries. This is particularly important for countries where IPR violations are rampant in key sectors and national laws are either weak or not enforced. United States and EU business executives and appropriate government agencies specific concerns about violations by third countries of intellectual property rights and make suggestions for improving their enforcement.

IV.4c The United States and EU should also strongly encourage advanced developing countries to accelerate the implementation of the TRIPs Agreement rather than taking the full transition period.

IV.5 Corruption and Bribery
The EU and the United States should give the highest priority to collective efforts to combat corruption and bribery, and fully support the prompt implementation of the 1994 OECD Recommendation on Bribery in International Transactions, including appropriate legislation

aimed at eliminating illicit payments, extortion and bribery, and including sanctions against such practices.

IV.6 Export Controls

The United States and the EU should provide all necessary support for the New Forum and take into account the views expressed in the joint business position adopted in July 1995 when the New Forum was developed. Industry emphasises that the "New Forum" should be implemented quickly to limit post-COCOM uncertainty.

IV.6a History has shown that unilateral sanctions are not effective. The United States and the EU should avoid using unilateral sanctions and should establish an international consultative process on the use of trade barriers or economic sanctions as mechanisms for forcing change in the proliferation policies and actions of third countries. The objective of such a consultative process would be to encourage effective multilateral cooperation and discourage extraterritorial application of unilateral measures that violate international norms.

IV.7 Labour, Environment, Human Rights

Regarding human rights and labour protection, careful attention should be paid to differing cultures, social structures and levels of development. Legitimate questioning of certain practices (child labour, absence of social protection, etc.) should not be construed and used to impose additional restrictions and barriers to trade from those developing countries.

IV.7a Regarding trade and environment, given that the WTO is working on these problems in preparation for the next ministerial meeting, to be held in Singapore in December 1996, we acknowledge that the WTO is the right forum to discuss these matters and that the voice of business associations should be taken into account. Environmental issues also should not be used as protectionist measures.

An important source of financial resources in the developing world is the World Bank. The United States and the EU should encourage the Bank to balance the economic and environmental issues in its decision making process on loans to less developed countries.

IV.8 Accession of new members to WTO

The United States and EU should require that all new countries that seek to accede to the World Trade Organisation do so on commercially viable terms. At the same time, the United States and EU should provide the technical assistance that these countries require in the course of the accession process.

IV.8a The United States and the EU should seek to harmonise their policies and adopt a commercially pragmatic approach towards the admission of new countries to the WTO, since these countries are going to represent a significant part of world trade in the near future. Their accessions should respect the rules and principles of the WTO on all matters, especially regarding their policies on investment, services, industrial planning, intellectual property rights and trading rights. The countries should also have comprehensive and commercially acceptable tariff schedules.

IV.9 Trade and Competition Policies
The United States and the EU should support work in the OECD toward the "international contestability of markets" -- markets that allow unimpaired market access for foreign goods, services, ideas, investments and business people -- so that they are able to benefit from the opportunity to compete in a market on terms equal or comparable to those enjoyed by local competitors.

IV.9a The United States and EU should urge all countries to agree to make market access a priority in applying competition laws and regulations. This should apply also to those OECD countries which still allow anti-competitive practices on the part of their companies competing on world markets. All countries should be encouraged to examine the structure and application of their competition policies in order to identify means to improve market access.

Bibliography

Barber, L., "Brussels Keeps Shut the Gates to the East," *The Financial Times*, 16 November 1995.

Barber, L., "EU Summit Warns US on Sanctions," *The Financial Times*, 24 June 1996.

Barber, L., "Fresh Meat from Europe's Stable," *The Financial Times*, 8 December 1994.

Brittan, L., *"The EU-US Relationship: Will it Last?,"* Speech to the American Club in Brussels, 27 April 1995.

Christopher, W., *"Charting a Transatlantic Agenda for the 21st Century,"* Speech by Secretary of State in Madrid on 2 June 1995.

Dale, R., "Marshall to Maastricht: US-European Relations Since World War II," *Europe*, 1995.

Dale, R., "America's Bullying Trade Tactics," *International Herald Tribune*, 11 June 1996.

de Jonquières, G., "Japan Takes Tougher Line In Chips Dispute With US," *The Financial Times*, 1 July 1996.

European Commission, *"Europe and the United States: The Way Forward,"* July 1995.

European Commission, *"Free Trade Areas: An Appraisal,"* Communication from the Commission to the Council, IP/95/215, 8 March 1995.

Feldstein, M., "The Defence of Europe: It Can't Be Done Alone," *The Economist*, 25 February 1995.

The Financial Times, "Brussels Trade Pacts 'Corrosive'," 9 February 1996.

The Financial Times, "US Polices Aegean 'While EU Sleeps'," 9 February 1996.

Garten Ash, T., "Bosnia in Our Future," *New York Review of Books*, 21 December 1995.

Gaster, R. and Prestowitz, C., *"Shrinking the Atlantic: Europe and the American Economy,"* North Atlantic Research, Inc., 1995.

Ginsberg, R., "US-EC Relations" in *The European Community and the Challenge of the Future*, ed. Juliet Lodge, St. Martin's Press, 1989.

Grant, C., *Delors: Inside the House That Jacques Built*, Nicholas Brealey, 1994.

Harrison, G., *"A New Transatlantic Initiative? US-EU Economic Relations in the Mid-1990s'*," CRS Report for Congress, 15 September 1995.

Harrison, G., *"CRS Report for Congress: US-European Union Trade and Investment,"* Congressional Research Service, The Library of Congress, 20 December 1994.

Henning R., "Europe's Monetary Union and the United States", *Foreign Policy*, Spring 1996.

International Herald Tribune, "EU Promotes Own Weapons," 26 January 1996.

Kahler, M., *Regional Futures and Transatlantic Economic Relations*, Council on Foreign Relations Press, 1995.

Klau, T., "Tackling the Structural Monologue," *European Voice*, 22-28 February 1996.

Krause, A., "Inside the New Europe," Harper Collins, 1991.

Krenzler, H.G. and Schomaker, A., "A New Transatlantic Agenda," *European Foreign Policy*, Vol. 1, No. 1, 1996.

Lawday, D., "The Return of the Habsburgs," Special Supplement to *The Economist*, 18 November 1995.

Lewis, F., "Atlantic Connections Begin to Fray," *International Herald Tribune*, 23 June 1995.

Marsh, D. (1995), "EMU Strain Begins to Show," *The Financial Times*, 17 January 1995.

Mortimer, E., "Eurostructures Under One Roof," *The Financial Times*, 3 May 1995.

Nelson, M. and Ikenberry, G. J. (1993), *"Atlantic Frontiers: A New Agenda for US-EC Relations,"* Carnegie Endowment for International Peace.

Peterson, J., "Clinton and America in the Clinton Era," *Journal of Common Market Studies*, Vol. 32, No. 3, 1994.

Sbragia, A., *"Transatlantic Relations: An Evolving Mosaic,"* Paper presented to a conference in Brussels on Policy-Making and Decision-Making in Transatlantic Relations, 3-4 May 1996.

Schott, J., *"Reflections on TAFTA,"* Unpublished Paper delivered before the Council on Foreign Relations, 19 June 1995.

Schwok, R., *"US-EC Relations in the Post-Cold War Era: Conflict or Partnership?,"* Westview Press, 1991.

The Economist, "A Ghost At the Feast," 19 February 1994.

The Economist, "More-or-less European Union," 26 August 1995.

The Economist, "The Case Against EMU," 13 June 1992.

The Economist, "The Old World's New World," Supplement, 13 March 1993.

The Economist, "The Politics of Peace," 1 April 1995.

The Wall Street Journal, "Commission Calls for EU's Rules to Cover Arms," 27-28 January 1996.

Winand, P., *Eisenhower, Kennedy, and the United States of Europe*, St. Martin's Press, 1993.

Wise, E., "Progress on Plans For Transatlantic Degree," *European Voice*, 6-12 June 1996.